This I Remember

RICHARD D. MOORE

Copyright © 2003 by Richard D. Moore.
Printed in the United States. All rights reserved.

ISBN: 1-58597-188-X

Library of Congress Control Number: 2003109478

A division of Squire Publishers, Inc.
4500 College Blvd.
Leawood, KS 66211
1/888/888-7696
www.leatherspublishing.com

I want to dedicate this book to:

My wonderful wife Lois,

my daughter and my three sons.

ACKNOWLEDGEMENTS

These little stories are a collection of some of the experiences I have had as I've traveled through life. They have been written erratically with sometimes several years between stories. Some names and places have been altered. The stories would never have emerged at all except for the help and support I have always received from the girl who took a reckless chance and married me when I was a young Marine Corps pilot in WW II. Since that time she has been the stabilizing influence guiding my life, and I attribute to her any measure of enjoyment these stories might bring to the reader. I also have to mention my daughter, Patricia Elbrecht, who like her mother Lois, is a great encourager, and Patricia's dear friend, Lynda Kittle. Without the three of their editing and spelling skills, these stories would resemble Egyptian hieroglyphics.

TABLE OF CONTENTS

Paint	1
Hacking Ties	21
McGinnis	37
Bart	51
The Peril of Progress	75
Johnny Green	85
Cousin Bob	89
One Eye	115
Charley	155
Buford	161
The Demise of Lester Foutch	167
The Trial of Riley Tooley	191
Skeeter	207
Ethics	213
Maudibel	221

Paint

MY GRANDSON DANIEL is proud of his new cowboy boots. He rode our old ranch horse, Teppo, to our house, and he was a bit proud of that, too. He's 11 years old and into horses at the moment. He had my old roughout saddle repaired, and Chad, his friend, and he rode Teppo and Sue over to show it to me. I gave him my old rifle boot for his saddle, and he had a dozen questions, like how to fasten it on the saddle, what would happen if he fired his rifle off Rocky, our other ranch horse, which side of the saddle to hang it on, questions like that. He asked me all about the old ranch horses we gave to his mother when we sold the ranch, which I liked best, Rocky or Teppo, and then he asked me what was the best horse I ever knew. That was an easy one. I told him it was my Paint horse that I had during my teenage years. He was not only the best horse I ever knew; he was my best friend. We both grew up together.

Paint was not a paint horse at all; he was a bay. Fred Kentner had owned his mother, and Fred's youngest girl, Jean, had named him Paint as a colt. Paint he always remained. I bought him from Fred when he was a gangly yearling and wasn't much to look at. Fred needed the money more than he needed the horse. Now Fred had a way of bragging on any livestock he wanted to sell, so if you bought his blind cow, you'd think it was the best blind cow there was in the whole country. He bragged on what a fine horse that yearling would make, and as a boy who wanted a horse, I could visualize Paint turning into a combination of Dan Patch and Man-O-War. I had seen Fred's mares; they were rather high strung like Fred, but they were fine horses. I never saw or knew who Paint's sire was. I don't remember how much we paid Fred, but it couldn't have been much. We didn't have much.

We had two work horses, Kit and Cap. Kit was a black mare and Cap a bay horse. A person could ride them, but they were draft horses and not very agile. They were good steady horses and good at plowing and dependable at all sorts of farm work, but I wasn't as interested in plowing as I was in just riding an agile horse. I wanted a horse I could ride like cowboys did, one that you could rope from, jump over fences, head cattle and do all of the things that cowboy horses are supposed to do.

I was reared in the city until I was 14 years old. We always visited the country during summer vacations, and I got to ride some farm horses during that time. Sometimes I'd get to ride my Uncle's mules, but I never rode enough to get very proficient, and I never rode a real riding horse.

It was the year my mother and two sisters moved to the farm from the city when we bought Paint. I was 14 years old at the time. It was the in-between years, that adolescent period in a person's life before the reality of experiences constricts your imagination into reasonable bounds. In my imagination that scraggly yearling was already a beautiful bay gelding and could out-run, out-jump and out-perform any horse in the whole world. I started riding him the next spring when he was two.

Paint was a solid bay with the exception of a white spot about three inches in diameter between his eyes. He had an indentation in the white spot to the right of center about the size of your thumb nail and half an inch in depth. He must have been born with it, as I never knew him to be injured. He weighed about 750 pounds when I started riding him, and when he got his mature growth, he never weighed over 900 pounds. When he walked, he looked as if he were stiff in his hind legs. He walked this way from the time he was a yearling. I think he was born gentle. Although I was green around horses, I never knew it and Paint didn't seem to mind. From the onset he led well, responded quickly to the bit, and patiently tolerated the boy who jumped on his back. I didn't have a saddle at the time, only a burlap sack as a saddle blanket, but in a very short period of time Paint and I were as inseparable as any Comanche brave and his warhorse.

It was in the heart of the great depression. We had a few young steers and heifers, but there was no market for them until the government started buying. The top price paid by the government was $20, and it took a good animal to bring that. We had about 15 or 20 cattle that were pasture fed, and we needed the money they would bring. We lived about 13 miles from West Plains where the government was buying. Back at that time there were very few trucks available. Cattle were still shipped on the railroad, and to get cattle to a shipping point they were driven there from the various farms.

So that's what Paint and I undertook. We started out early one summer morning, and Paint took it in stride as if he had been driving cattle for years. It was about four miles from our barn lot to 63 highway. I tried not to drive them too fast so they wouldn't look gaunt when we reached the government buyer. Traffic on the highway wasn't so heavy back then. The automobile drivers were accustomed to seeing cattle being driven to town from time to time, and most were courteous in slowing their vehicles and easing past them. I don't remember anyone honking or trying to scare the cattle.

Paint was magnificent. If one of the herd tried to break ranks or turn down an open gate, with a touch of my heels he would burst forth like a rocket and head that miscreant back into the herd, and then whirl and be back driving the herd in a flash.

As we arrived in West Plains and approached Grace Avenue where the highway entered the city, we could hear the cattle bawling at the stockyards. Here the herd quickened their pace and were soon running pell-mell across yards and gardens toward the sound; Paint and I were in close pursuit. As we turned down St. Louis street toward the stockyard, the noise reached a crescendo. Penned cattle were bawling; new cattle arriving, including ours, joined in the chorus; workers and herdsmen were yelling and penning cattle, and it seemed as if all were confusion and bewilderment. Out of that cacophony of confusion, however, there emerged an order not apparent at first. Workers emerged out of the melee who took over the driving and direction of the herd, shouting orders to gate men who assisted them in penning the cattle and tagging them. The old stockyards were located east of where Richard's store is located today, and I heard no complaints from the townspeople whose yard and gardens were trampled. They seemed to take it in stride as if they were used to having cattle run across their yards once in a while. At least I heard no complaints. I watered Paint at the watering trough, tied him to a hitching post, and waited for the government buyer to price the cattle. They brought close to top dollar, and when I swaggered over to Pirnack's grocery store to buy a dime's worth of crackers and longhorn cheese, I am certain no cattle baron ever felt more pride when he ordered prime rib in Dodge City after his cattle drive from Texas. Paint would patiently wait for his feed until we went back to the farm. Paint was two years old at the time. I was 15. It was our first cattle drive.

We had about 18 or 20 head of nondescript cows which I milked as long as I could squeeze a cup of milk from them. We had what they called a cold water separator. We would draw cold water from the well, put it in the separator along with the milk and in the morning draw the cream off. The sale of the cream provided a little grocery money. The county was divided into ranges. Some were what was called open range and some were closed range. In open range you were free to pasture your livestock on the open range outside of your farm. All of this open range consisted of woodland and road right-of-way where the cattle could get a little wild grass. We were in open range and we pastured in the woods. To the north of our place there were about 1500 acres of open land, and this is where our cows grazed during the spring, summer and fall months. Of course, some of our neighbors utilized this open range also.

We put bells on our cows so we could locate them in the woods, as we had to gather them every night to milk them. We lotted them at night, milked them in the morning again and turned them back out in the woods. This system wasn't conducive to much milk production on the part of the cows, but on the plus side it didn't require a cash outlay of any kind. And cash was what we didn't have. Of course. our neighbors followed the same basic procedure. and they would bell their cows also to locate them. You quickly became able to discern your own cowbells and learn to know your cows from your neighbors'.

Paint soon was able to pick out our bells from the others. I would ride to the top of a hill and wait to hear the bells. Often Paint would hear them before I did and head for them. In the hot summer the cows dreaded to walk that hot trail back to the farm. They knew about what time we would be coming after them, and they would stand very still under some thick undergrowth so their bells wouldn't ring. Then Paint would stand patiently until the flies would penetrate the cows' cover. The bell cows would throw their heads back to chase the flies from their back, and you'd briefly hear the bells clang. That's all it would take for Paint. When he heard the first clang or tingle of a bell, he headed straight for the cow. He would urge the laggard along by nipping her on the tail.

It was before the bulldozer had made its appearance, and most of the farm ponds were made by what was called a slip pulled by two horses or mules. The ponds were small, and most of them dried up in the hot summer months. A few natural ponds, those that had formed when a large sink compacted to the extent it would hold water, existed, and they were a salvation to the cattle during dry weather. When we heard a symphony of bells coming from the vicinity of the John West pond, as it was called, we'd head there and locate them quickly.

Driving cattle every day, Paint soon became a very proficient cow horse. He could almost anticipate what a cow would do. He could also anticipate what I wanted to do and would respond to the slightest touch of my heels or shift of my weight. I soon could cut any animal out of the herd, or head the fastest steer while riding Paint without saddle or bridle. His speed was deceptive, partly because he didn't look fast. When he walked, he still looked as if he were stiff in his hindquarters. He developed sort of a little running walk, but when he walked normally in the field or down the road that stiffness was noticeable. Ev Ball, a friend, bought a blooded mare named Beulah that had all the looks of a sleek and powerful runner. Every once in a while Ev would have occasion to ride Beulah with Paint and me. On several occasions he challenged us to a race, and Paint won every time. Ev soon quit even trying.

Paint learned to jump, not real high, but he could clear a four-foot obstacle. He could hold any steer or horse tied to the saddle horn, and he learned to step over fences when they were pressed down for him. That saved both of us a great deal of time. I would tie a pair of knippers and a hammer by the saddle strings, and we would ride straight across country. If we came to a fence, I'd loosen the staples, lower the fence wire, and Paint would step over. Then I'd restaple the fence as good as new. All of my neighbors knew I did this, and as long as I put the fence back as it was, they didn't care. Paint's ability became legend about the neighborhood, and when any of the neighbors had an animal they couldn't corral, they'd come looking for Paint and me. Riding as much as I did entailed putting shoes on Paint about every two weeks. I couldn't ride the 13 miles to town every time he needed shoeing, so I learned to tack shoes on him, and soon I was in great demand by my neighbors to shoe their horses.

Once in a while we'd ride with other riders, but most of the time we traveled alone. We went fishing quite often and explored the countryside. On one such occasion I was riding by a dry creek bed west of my brother-in-law's place when I came to an opening in the bed of the creek. I tied Paint to a bush and went down to explore. The opening turned out to be a cave the water had carved into limestone. I entered and found myself crawling along a narrow opening. I had no matches or flashlight, and soon I was crawling on my hands and knees in total darkness. I felt the path abruptly end when one of my hands suddenly found only air beneath it. I grasped around and found a small rock, and then reached out and dropped it to see if I could tell how steep the drop-off was. I know it wasn't long, but it seemed as if it was an interminable time before I heard a "plunk" far below. I didn't waste any time backing out, and was real happy to see daylight again. A few weeks later, I was going by the same creek and decided to ride back to look at the hole. It had all caved in. I could imagine what would have happened if the cave-

Paint

in had occurred when I happened to be inside. Paint would have been found tied to a bush, and my disappearance would have been forever a mystery. I have always been a bit apprehensive of caves since, and never again ventured into one alone.

During the school term I rode the school bus to Koshkonong High School, which was about 14 miles down the road from our place. Extracurricular school activity was rare, as most of the bussed students were farm kids and had chores to do after school. Few had their own transportation. Every once in a while though, during a successful basketball season, the bus would make a night run to pick up students for a game. In that way the team was assured of a good cheering section, and the rural students who were on the team would have a ride home. These were special occasions that the students looked forward to with anticipation, and I was no exception. On those occasions the school bus would leave the school just a trifle early, so the students could get their chores over with in time to ride the bus back to the game.

One such night, I came home from school and hurried to milk my cows. I had trouble finding one that was due to calf. When I finally found her and finished milking the other, I knew I would probably miss the bus. Before I had cleaned up, the bus came, honked once and, when I didn't promptly go running out, pulled off. I felt crushed with the bitter disappointment only experienced during the teenage years, when some trivial event seems of momentous importance at the time. In my moment of desperation, I ran to the barn lot and threw a saddle on Paint. If I could cut through the timber, I could get ahead of the bus six miles from our place at Brandsville and ride the bus on to Koshkonong and see the game.

The night was dark, but Paint was sure-footed and galloped through the trees. We finally came to the road to Brandsville well ahead of the bus, and I rode Paint to the intersection of the Brandsville road and the highway. I tied Paint to a post at an old filling station my uncle used to own and caught the bus. There Paint patiently stood until the bus returned close to midnight. It was the talk of the neighborhood how Paint had beaten the school bus to Brandsville — rather tantamount to the Midnight Ride of Paul Revere. Both of us arrived home well after midnight. Both of us were weary. Both of us were young. Paint was three, and I was 16.

The years passed. In the spring of 1936, my father, who had been ill for some time, passed away. We looked forward with hope to the price of livestock increasing, so we had purchased some two-year-old heifers from Zonrow Trantham at what I thought was a bargain. I was not that experienced, but was beginning to be able to come fairly close to evaluating the weight and quality of an animal. We bought the heifers after Dad died and turned them out on the open range. We put the bottom field in corn and cleaned out an old pit silo and filled it with silage for the cows and young heifers for winter feed. As it turned out, the summer corn crop produced well. With the silo filled, we looked forward to the spring crop of calves. When Dad died, he had a small insurance policy, but the company went bankrupt, so we were in need of a profit on the cattle.

The winter was hard. I was inexperienced. When I put the corn in the silo and one of the neighbors, who had never put up any silage of his own, told me I should put water with the corn, I added water. As a result, the silage was of poor quality. We didn't have the money to buy protein supplement, and I didn't know anything about credit, or have anyone I thought I could turn to for advice. My mother depended on me, and I couldn't tell her how inadequate I felt as I watched spring approaching with the cattle getting weaker. Paint became my confidant, and I'd have long, one-sided conversations with Paint. In the spring when we began to lose some of the heifers because they were too weak to calve, Paint would stand patiently by while I skinned the carcass to get the three or four dollars the hide would bring. Only Paint would see me cry.

The next year the price of cattle did pick up and, in spite of the winter's loss, made a little money.

In the late spring, Paint got an infection in his left front hoof. It happened very quickly. One day he was limping; by the next day, his leg was so swollen it was twice its normal size. I had my neighbor, Lee Morrison, look at it, and he told me I had better get a veterinarian as soon as possible. The only veterinarian in the county at that time was Dr. Ted Wilkie, and he drove out as soon as I went to see him. He prescribed soaking Paint's hoof in some warm water with disinfectant. In addition, he gave me some powder to put in his feed. It was before antibiotics were discovered, and I never learned what was in the powder. Wilkie was always concocting some medicine and labeling it with his name and stating on the label what it was for. Whether it was the soaking or the powder or both, something worked.

I soaked Paint's hoof day and night for two days. I

would take food and water to him and change the warm disinfectant water in the pail he was soaking his foot in as soon as it began to cool. He seemed to know I was trying to help him, for he never tried to get his foot out of the pail. About the third day the swelling began to subside, and within a week his leg was almost normal, but he could not be ridden for another month.

In the late fall of 1937 our old draft mare, Kit, died from founder. That left us without a team. Paint had never worn a harness, but we had no alternative than to see if we could pair Paint up with our draft horse, Cap. Cap was a rather large, stocky-built draft animal and weighed a good 300 pounds more than Paint, and we didn't know if they could work together. We didn't need to be concerned. Paint worked with Cap as if he had worn harness all his life. What he lacked in weight, he made up in sheer nerve and heart. He would pull as much and as long as Cap.

In the spring of 1938, we began to hear that there was opportunity for work in California. After much discussion, Mother decided to take the car and see if she could get work from some connections she had there. I would stay and look after the farm, and my younger sister would stay with my older married sister who lived with her husband on a farm a couple miles from our place. That left Paint as my only means of transportation. Paint and I managed just fine. When I needed to go to town, I'd go with a neighbor or ride over to my brother-in-law's place and either ride with him or borrow his pickup.

It was a time of camaraderie when young and old made their own entertainment. Young people would gather at the one-room schoolhouse on Saturday night and play their guitars and sing or perform skits or little plays. We had neighborhood rodeos that Paint and I always participated in, and we had carnivals which would draw people from several miles around. We didn't have nor need much money for amusement. A nickel or a dime would buy enough ice to make ice cream for a gathering.

During this period of time I began to buddy with Harry Chapin. Harry was the younger brother of my sister's husband, and he lived with my sister and brother-in-law. Harry and I would ride our horses together and on occasion would break horses for some of our neighbors. On one occasion we rode to a rodeo at Thayer, which was about 20 miles from our place. We didn't get home until early the next day.

At one of our neighborhood carnivals, I happened to get together with Harry's cousin, Lois. She was a beautiful blond-haired girl whom I had known for several years, but had never had the opportunity to get very well acquainted with. She lived several miles closer to town than we did, and we would rarely be in the same group.

As Winston Churchill said, "History turns on fine agate points." It happened to be a chilly evening. I happened to be wearing a sweater and she had none, so I volunteered mine. She accepted and wore my sweater during the evening. It was a simple as that. She was a very lovely and popular girl. She had a number of suitors, all of whom had vehicles, who were ready, willing and anxious to escort her various places. It was unusual for her to be unescorted, and it was unusual for her to appear at this country carnival, but there she was. I still don't know how she happened to be there.

At any rate, we got into somebody's pickup to get out of the chill; I don't remember whether it was my brother-in-law's or not. I wasn't paying any attention to the pickup. I don't remember what we talked about. All I remember is that the evening passed so quickly that it was soon time for her to go home. I don't remember whether she left with her brother or whether she had driven the family's car by herself.

That was the start of my going with Lois. She was close to her cousin Harry. They had been reared on adjoining farms and had gone to school together. She liked to ride horseback, and before long Harry, Lois and I were riding horseback together, and sometimes we'd borrow my brother-in-law's pickup and we'd all three go to town together. On some occasions Harry would get a date, and the four of us would go out together. Sometimes we'd get another horse for Harry's girl, and the four of us would ride together. Lois didn't seem to mind that I didn't have a car like the other fellows she had been going with. Sometimes, I'd borrow my brother-in-law's car and we would go out just by ourselves. When I would take the pickup back late in the night, Paint would be patiently waiting, and I'd talk the evening over with him as we traveled the two miles home.

I had been out of high school over two years when I decided to go to the University. It was a decision based on desire rather than reality, as I had no concept of what was involved. I had known some friends and relatives who had attended the Missouri Teachers College in Springfield to get a teaching certificate, but they generally had a teaching job, or were promised one. I wanted to go to the University at Columbia. I did not know anyone in Columbia or anyone going to school there, how much it would cost, or really what I was interested in studying. I just wanted to go. I had no money. All I had was the desire and encouragement of my mother and sisters, so I began planning in that direction.

In the spring of '39 I contacted a distant cousin, Fred Ball, who was looking for work. Fred was newly married and, like the rest of us, having a rough time financially. I made an arrangement with him to move into our house and take care of the livestock for a share of the sale of the proceeds. By this time farm prices had risen, we had accumulated a fair-sized herd and several horses. Paint was still our mainstay. Fred was a hard-working, honest and dependable person, about my age, and I had no hesitation about turning the house and farm over to his care.

With the care of the farm arranged for, I applied for admission to the University and submitted a transcript of my high school credits. There was some difficulty when they discovered I lacked four years of high school credits. I had graduated from the eighth grade in Omaha in December of 1932. In Omaha they had the school semesters divided into two parts, and I had graduated from grade school at the end of the fall semester. I had gone immediately to Missouri and entered high school at Brandsville as a freshman and in the spring passed to the sophomore class. The Brandsville High School then closed for lack of funds. Most of the students went to Koshkonong the next year. I went the last year to West Plains, and there it was discovered that my transcript was lacking one half year of showing a four-year attendance. They never asked me for an explanation, but concluded a half year's transcripts had been lost when the Brandsville records were transferred to Koshkonong. I never enlightened them, and I was graduated from West Plains High School in three and one-half years. The University accepted West Plains' explanation and approved my transcript. I was notified that I was eligible to attend the fall semester of 1939.

It was the summer before I started in the University that I spent every evening I could with Lois. Most of the time I would ride to my brother-in-law's place and borrow his pickup. Sometimes Harry would go with us, but increasingly we would go by ourselves. The summer passed so quickly, it was time for me to leave before I had hardly time to prepare. But leave I did, turning the farm and livestock over to Fred. I hitched a ride with our sheriff who was taking a prisoner to Jefferson City; then, when he volunteered to take me the extra 20 miles to Columbia, I didn't object. With all my belongings in a small suitcase and $100 in my pocket, the sheriff let me off at the campus in Columbia. Paint quickly became a distant memory. Paint was 7; I was 20.

There was an air of uncertainty that hung over the country. Germany invaded Poland in the fall, and the aura of impending war was in the air. I attended the University for a couple of years. During the spring of 1941 I enrolled in a Civilian Pilot Training course and obtained my private pilot's license. When the spring semester ended in '41, I left Columbia and went to join my mother in California. With the U.S. supporting England and its allies through the lend lease program, production began to pick up over the entire country. Fred Ball wrote that he wanted to get a job in the de-

Paint

fense plant; so, in the latter part of the summer of '41, Mother and I drove home and sold our belongings, including livestock and furniture at the farm, on the auction block. I don't even remember who bought Paint or how he left the farm. Paint was 9; I was 22. Before driving back to California, I stopped to see Lois for a few minutes in Gainsville where she was working.

With war declared in '42, I enlisted in the Navy Flight Program and trained until the fall of '43. When I was to be commissioned in the Marine Corps, I sent a telegram to the girl I had courted on Paint, the girl who didn't seem to mind that I didn't have a car like her other suitors had. We had been separated three years and had corresponded rather infrequently, but she took a train to Corpus Christi, Texas, for my commissioning. After a few days of getting reacquainted, we were married there. I still didn't have a car.

I returned home in the late fall of 1945 and was separated from service in the first part of '46. We moved back to the farm and remodeled the old farm house; I studied law, passed the bar, ran for and served several terms as prosecuting attorney, and we had three children going to school by 1957.

One summer evening when I returned home from the office, the children told me about an old horse that had come and tried to get in the yard at a place where the gate used to be before we remodeled the house. When I asked them where the horse was now, they said it went up the hill, toward the Bach place to the south. I didn't think any more of it until the next day. When I drove up, the children were out in the yard and an old thin horse was just going around the back of the house. I could only see his hindquarters, and what I saw brought back a flood of memories. There was no mistaking that same stiff walk in his hindquarters. I knew immediately it was Paint. With my heart racing, I jumped out of the car and followed him to a feed trough at the back of the yard. Overjoyed at seeing my old friend, I ran and grabbed him by the neck and hugged him. I felt the indentation in the white spot on his forehead. He was skin and bones, but he was Paint. I told him that we'd see that he'd have enough to eat and soon he would be poor and thin no longer. Paint was 25, I was 39.

I told the children to watch the horse, and I went to town to get some sweet horse feed. I purchased the feed and came home as quickly as I could. I put the feed up and poured a half-gallon in the trough for Paint. He was famished and grabbed the biggest mouthful he could. He seemed to have trouble chewing it and rolled it around in his mouth, slobbering, and then tried to swallow it without chewing. He immediately choked. Feed and saliva came pouring out of his mouth and nostrils. He never took another bite, but instead turned from the trough as in resignation. He walked a few feet from the trough and just stood there. The next morning he was still in about the same spot.

I contacted Dr. Clark, and he came and looked at Paint. Doc said that when Paint choked on the feed he got some in his lungs and contracted mechanical pneumonia. There was no cure for mechanical pneumonia. The next day when I came home, Paint was gone. The children said he had gone up the hill toward the Bach place. I drove to the Bach Place, which was the name for the south part of our farm, and there lay Paint. He had evidently quietly laid down and died.

I was curious where he had come from and inquired around. I learned that some people had seen an old horse working his way up from Arkansas for several weeks. I never did learn just where he started from.

Several weeks later I still couldn't get Paint off my mind, and I drove up to the Bach place once again to see my old friend. The scavengers had done their work. One look at the skeleton of his head revealed what his problem had been. Two long jaw teeth had prevented his teeth from coming together enough for him to chew his food. It is a common problem in older horses. It is also a problem that can nearly always be helped by "floating" the teeth. Floating is done by rasping the offending teeth down evenly with the others.

Our days of youth began to flood my mind in a cascade of memories: The moonlight rides, the cattle drives, the rides on a hot summer day to the cool creek, the riding over the color-splashed autumn countryside picking ripe and juicy Indian peaches and apples. Paint could reach back and pick an apple out of my hand while traveling at a gallop. I suddenly had the sense of helplessness similar to what flooded over me when our cattle began dying after that hard winter of '36-'37. Paint had traveled back to the scenes of his youth for help from the boy who had soaked his foot, and I felt that I had failed him. I should have realized what his problem was, but I had failed. Once again only Paint saw me cry.

Hacking Ties

IT'S FUNNY HOW ONE thing sometimes leads to another. Fent Dixon stopped by one morning and told me about some of the neighborhood fellows meeting every Friday morning over a cup of coffee and solving the ills of the world. He asked me to join them and put in my contribution, figuring maybe I'd have a better solution than Al Gore. I thought I'd have a better one, too, so one morning I went.

One of the fellows in attendance was Don Featherston. I had known Don years ago when I first started high school at Brandsville. Don was younger than I, and I didn't know him very well, but I was well acquainted with some of his older brothers and sisters. When you're 14, you don't pay much attention to a kid three years younger than you. When you're 80, those three years don't seem to matter.

The name Featherston seemed to strike a bell in my mind. I remembered when I returned home from WW II and reorganized the local National Guard, we were sent to Fort Leonard Wood for our first summer camp. There I met a number of weekend warriors from various parts of the State. One young officer from Ripley

County was named Featherston, Jim Featherson. Jim was an engaging fellow with an easygoing nature, a repertoire of risqué jokes, and a rather cavalier approach to life in general, and to military life in particular.

It turned out that Don and Jim were double cousins. Don brought me a book Jim had had published which was a compilation of his experiences growing up and living in Ripley County. The stories ranged the gauntlet from his early education in a one-room school to his service as the county sheriff at a tender age. They were well written and amusing. I obtained his address from Don and wrote him a letter. He responded quickly and presented me with a subscription to a rural paper he writes for occasionally.

One of his stories concerned apprehending timber thieves, who constituted a nuisance in his jurisdiction when he was sheriff. There were large areas in his part of the Ozarks devoted to the growing of timber. Most of these tracts were owned by timber companies, the railroad, the government or some other entity. This made most of the timber grown fair game for a good portion of the good citizens of the county. A number of the more enterprising citizens developed quite a proficiency in the ancient art of using a broadax, and they turned that art into the making of ties and selling them to the railroad. You might say it developed into a cottage industry in counties like Ripley. A couple of these artists could slip in and hack a load of ties, load them on their old truck, and have them sold at the tie yard before their worthy opponents, who were duty bound to keep this from happening, had their second cup of morning coffee. In this manner they contributed to the general economy, augmented their government checks, kept the quality of their coon dogs top notch, and enabled them to buy some extra molasses for the kids.

My sympathies were inclined to be with the hackers for reasons I'll relate to you later, and I conveyed this to Jim. He wrote back disparagingly about a broadax, calling it that "crooked-handled" old thing. I responded by writing him that I thought the reason for his bad memories was that he had never used an ax with a straight handle. That's what I mean about one thing leading to another. It took me back in my memories sixty-some odd years to a different time in a different world.

The winter of 1936-37 was a cold one in more ways than one. My father died the 1st of May in '36. He had a small life insurance policy, but the company took bankruptcy like so many companies did during that time. Previously he worked for the Union Pacific Railroad in Omaha, Nebraska, and his wages kept the family fairly comfortable while he was able to work. He became ill several years before his death; and in 1932, when I turned 14 and graduated from grade school, he sent me down to live with some of my mother's people in rural Howell County. In 1935, my mother, two sisters and our household furniture arrived at our old farmhouse. It was in the fall of 1935 that Doc Boone showed up one evening.

Now, it was a different world we lived in back then. We had no locks on our doors and neither did our neighbors. If you were fixing fence and left your crow bar and your post maul where you stopped working, you could go back a year from then, dig through the weeds and find them.

People traveling through the country, on occasion,

would stop and ask for sleeping accommodations for the night and were seldom turned away. So I was not surprised one evening in early fall to find a fellow I would have judged to be in his late fifties knocking on the door, asking if he could stay the night. He asked if Cousin Mirthey lived there, and said his name was Doc Boone. He also announced in a matter of fact way, as if it was a common occurrence, that he had just gotten out of the "bug house." Evidently ours was the first house he had honored with his presence. Now as easy-going and hospitable as we were back then, it was the first time I had ever had someone ask to stay the night and announce right off that he had just gotten out of the "bug house."

I had never heard the term "mental illness." In my limited experience a person was either sane or they were nuts. When someone spoke of illness, it meant you were sick, probably with a fever, which you cured with an onion poultice or a dose of castor oil or both. If you were nuts, you went to the County Farm or the State Hospital, which was termed, in rough vernacular, as the "bug house." It was before Freud had invaded our drawing rooms. Psychologists and psychiatrists were just difficult words to spell. They weren't real people who could actually do something. It was the age of innocence before the legal profession took illusion and turned it into something concrete by conjuring up the "expert witness."

Doc looked okay, and outside of speaking of the "bug house" in an off-hand manner like getting out or being in was no big deal, he seemed as sane as the rest of our neighbors. I thought I could see a bit of resemblance to the Pentecost side of the family in his features, and he wanted to see Cousin Mirthey. My mother's name was Mirtha. Her mother's family had come from the Kentucky-Tennessee area in their migration from the East to Missouri, and I knew they would recognize a cousin back at least 10 generations before they were cut off from the family tree. So I called mother from the kitchen and, sure enough, she remembered Doc from about 20 years back.

Doc, it seemed, a number of years ago had a dispute with his wife and a neighbor or two in which he had threatened to kill them and made some overt act toward accomplishing his intentions, so he had been bundled up by the local constabulary and sent to the State Asylum at Nevada, Missouri. Once incarcerated there, it seemed no one was interested in his release except Doc, and he languished there for a number of years before he was released. I don't know how he found our house or how he arrived. He just showed up.

Well, he partook of supper with us, and Mother fixed him a place to sleep in the loft. The next morning we ate breakfast, and Doc asked what we needed done. That was all there was to it. He just assumed he had found a home and work. I discussed it with Mother, and we concluded we'd let him stay for a while and he could help with the work for his room and board. In the meantime, we'd keep a close watch on his actions to see if he was "all right." After all, he seemed harmless enough. Doc on his part was apparently gratified to have a roof over his head and food at mealtime. There was no talk from him or us about any payment for his labor. There simply wasn't any money to pay if we wanted to. What little cash we had went for food and the necessities of life. Knowing this, Doc accepted and respected the circumstances.

Doc was what I would call a medium-sized man, about 5' 10" tall, with a large nose, and with kind of a protruding forehead. He had tiny, squinty blue eyes that revealed the Cherokee blood that many of mother's relatives carried, and he walked in a way that I would call deliberate. That's a funny way of putting it, but that's the best way I can describe it. He never seemed to be in a hurry. I never saw him run, but I never saw him hesitate either. It seemed as if he had figured out beforehand where he was going and set out in a deliberate way to get there. He possessed many skills, skills that have been lost with the years, skills like riving boards to shingle a roof, stripping strips of white oak to weave baskets, parching field corn, baking corn pone, making all sorts of handles, hewing with a broadax, and he was an artist with a double-bitted ax. It wasn't because he was fast or even extra strong that he could get so much accomplished in the woods. It was, just like his walking, because of the deliberate way he went about it. He used a heavy ax, kept it razor sharp, could chop either right-handed or left-handed, and made every lick count. In the course of a day he could clear a pretty good patch of woods. I was a stout 18-year-old at the time, and was stronger at lifting, quicker, and thought I could get a lot done, but I couldn't hold a candle to Doc. In his steady, deliberate way he would just accomplish more, whether plowing or clearing, than I could.

As I related at the onset, the winter of '36-'37 was a cold one. Wood was the source of our heat, a wood cook stove in the kitchen and a King heater for the other two rooms in the house. Wood was plentiful, so we kept warm enough when we were inside, but our few old milk cows that we depended on for cream to sell began to dry up and so did the little cash we had to buy the necessities of life, like food, corn meal, kerosene for lamps and other luxuries. One bitter cold night when the snow was swirling past the window, the wind was howling, and the King stove was fairly jumping, we began to take stock of the situation at hand and discuss various possibilities. Doc had parched some hickory cane corn as an after-supper snack and we were munching on it. You know, it's almost impossible to crush the spirit of the entrepreneur when his body is warm and his stomach's full, and Doc allowed that we could make pretty good if we'd hack a load of ties and sell them to the railroad.

I demurred, pointing out that I was not only inept with an ax, but a broadax had never graced my hands. Doc stuck some homegrown tobacco into his pipe and allowed he could show me how. I was still dubious, but my resistance was getting weaker. "All we have is knotty post oak, and they'd make good posts, but I don't think they'd make good ties. Besides, most of the ties I've seen at the yard are sawed," I related.

"Post oak makes good ties," Doc responded with the air of one with superior knowledge. The King heater and supper had done its work. My resistance was at a low ebb. I was ripe for the plucking, so it was settled then and there. We would reverse our monetary fortunes by hacking a load of ties and selling them to the railroad. We turned in with the visions of anticipated revenues jingling in our pockets.

The next morning the new snow was over a foot in depth and the temperature was a shivery zero degrees. I could look out the window, glazed with frost, and see the post oaks behind the house standing silently, tauntingly, silhouetted against the snow, just daring any mere mortal to rip their frozen body with saw or ax. If Doc shared my apprehension, he didn't show it, but was even a bit exuberant as we fed the cows and chopped holes in the pond so they could get water. After breakfast we resolutely gathered our tools and set forth to turn those post oaks into railroad ties.

Our house was at the base of a rather large hill that rose to the south. It was on the north side of this hill that a number of large post oak trees grew, and it was there that Doc and I made our assault. Our tools were simple. They consisted of what we called a ribbon cross-cut saw, which we had borrowed from a neighbor, two double-bitted axes, a couple of wedges, a maul and a broadax. It didn't take long to discover that our cross-cut saw had not been sharpened in some time, and trying to cut into the frozen trunk of a tough post oak with that dull saw reminded me of stories I had read about prisoners digging their way out of dungeons with a pewter spoon. It did not help matters that I had not worked with a saw or an ax to any great extent. I had been introduced to these tools when I had first arrived in Missouri, but I hadn't used them enough to become very proficient. This quickly became apparent when I began working one end of the saw.

Doc would complain, "Stop dragging your feet!" as he worked the saw. I would grunt and struggle, back aching, feet, hands, nose and ears freezing, and body sweating as I tried to overcome my lack of skill with muscle and effort. After an interminable time, our persistence was rewarded and the giant was slain. It was too cold for us to savor our victory for very long. If we stopped to rest our weary muscles, the sweat our body generated began to chill, so we had to keep moving. Besides, once we had the tree down, our work had just begun. You see, before the day of the chain saw, the branches were taken off a tree with an ax. The only advantage of the ax over the saw was that our axes were sharp, and I found it much easier to swing an ax than to pull a dull saw. Then, you had to cut the trunk in eight-foot sections to make a tie. From the first tree we felled, we cut two eight-foot sections after we had chopped off the branches.

Then began the task of hacking the log into a tie, which I discovered was another thing completely unrelated to anything I had attempted to do before. If the invention of the chain saw was brought about by someone who had been condemned to fell frozen post oaks with a dull saw, as I firmly believe, the circle saw was invented by someone condemned to attempt to make a rectangular piece of timber from a log with a broadax. The face of the ax itself is from 12 to 15 inches in length, shaped like the pictures you see of the old executioner's axes, sharpened on one side only so as to present a flat surface to the log you are wanting to square. It had a crook in the handle near the head that enabled a skilled user to hew a smooth flat surface. One other characteristic I shouldn't omit — it was heavy.

Doc had used a broadax some time back, but he was out of practice. I had never had one in my hands before. However, he was a patient teacher. He explained the principles and demonstrated to the best of his ability. He taught me how to score the log with the chopping ax, which was cutting the side of the log at 8 to 10-inch intervals to the depth of the line that would constitute one side of the tie. This would enable the broadax user to cut or hack a smoother surface. Scoring the log was a rather simple procedure, but again it took a bit of skill. If you didn't cut the side deep enough, it wouldn't help the broadax user, and if you cut it too deep your cuts would mar the surface the broadax made. I grasped the principle quickly enough, but applying it took a bit longer. But, again, Doc was patient. I was the only help he had available and he was committed.

It took us all day to square up one tie. The next day we did better. We sawed down another tree and this time we hacked one tie and part of another one. It was still as cold as the day before, and we were glad to quit when evening came. The weather moderated some, but it never rose above freezing; however, our efficiency began to improve. We borrowed a file from our neighbor from whom we had borrowed the saw, and sharpened it. I began to acquire more skill at scoring. I even branched out by trying my hand some with the broadax. Doc would generally have to straighten out the side I'd worked on, but I thought I was coming along in pretty good shape. Our efficiency improved to two ties a day, then three. In the course of a week and a half we had ties scattered over the hillside and figured we had enough to make a load.

I was the business agent for the enterprise, so I was responsible for securing a truck to haul the load some 13 miles away to the tie yard in West Plains. The only truck I knew of was the one owned and used by our cream and milk hauler, Noah Wilson, who lived in the little town of Brandsville some six miles from our place. So one night in about the middle of the week, I drove to Brandsville after we had finished feeding to seek out Noah Wilson. Noah was an entrepreneur in his own right. At a time when there were very few trucks in our part of the country, Noah had procured a truck and started a cream and egg route, taking farmer's produce to market in West Plains. Later when a company put in a milk producing plant, he added milk pickup. At this particular time the cold weather had slowed his farm produce pickups to a trickle and he was running his route only two or three time a week, so he welcomed any additional business that came his way. We had no phones, so without any advance notice I knocked on his door one night. Noah and his wife had been sitting by the stove when he answered my knock and invited me to come in and sit. Noah was sober.

Noah was in his early 40s, a man of medium build and pleasant personality. I explained my mission and he was ready to help. He agreed, come Saturday, he'd bring his truck to our place and take our ties to the tie yard in West Plains to be sold. That was it. No haggling or question about price, it was a simple contract with no provisos. Both of us knew without mention that the charges would be both reasonable and fair. I left with mission accomplished, and a hope that the weather would be merciful come Saturday.

Saturday dawned, cold and overcast with a cutting wind but no snow. Also with the dawn came Noah. The ties were scattered about the hillside, and we had to cut a path for the truck. It took a bit of planning since we had to keep the truck aimed downhill as we loaded to keep it from getting stuck. Noah helped us load the ties and worked as hard as we did. In later years I've heard skiers describe a ski run as exhilarating, but I don't think their experience can compare to the exhilaration I experienced when we finally got all the ties on the truck and made it down to the main road. If you've ever tried to carry an eight-foot post oak tie on your shoulder, you know what I mean, it's more than a relief to get it off — it's positively exhilarating.

It was about 12 noon when we finally were loaded and ready to go to town. Doc was staying and keeping the fire stoked and feeding the cattle in the evening. I went with Noah to help him unload the ties. Noah's truck was bare bones — no radio, no heater — but it didn't matter. My ears, nose, toes and fingers might freeze, but my heart was warm and eager with anticipation. We were headed to town with a cargo as precious as that which had ever graced the hold of a Spanish galleon.

The tie yard was located on Washington Avenue adjacent to the railroad tracks on the west side of the street. I noticed that all the other loads coming in were sawed ties. Ours was the only load that had been hewed. I looked up the tie buyer and directed him to our load for his inspection. There was something about the way he looked at the load that filled me with trepidation. He didn't start tallying up the number as he did with the other loads, but instead walked to first one side of the truck then to the other. After pausing as if to consider, he made the announcement that sent my hopes, which had been soaring, to the border of despair. "Kid, we can't take these, they're all culls," he remarked. I am certain that no judgment ever pronounced had a more apocalyptic message to the ears of the hearer.

I'm sure I stuttered, but I finally overcame the shock and managed to stammer, "I really need to sell these bad. Won't you give me anything for them?" I thought I saw a flicker of compassion flash in his eyes for a split second, but they were dashed against the shoals when he answered, "Naw, kid, we can't use these, but you might be able to get them by up at Pomona where they're buying."

Noah had been privy to the conversation and, quickly appraising the situation, said, "Dick, if we hurry to Pomona, we might get there before they close."

The buyer by now had turned to go back to the warmth of his buyer's cabin, so I jumped in the cab of the truck and away we went to Pomona. It was another 12 miles of rattling and shivering. This time I was more acutely aware that my ears, nose, toes and fingers were freezing, as I was lacking the euphoria of expectation that had warmed me on our way to West Plains. The euphoria had been replaced by an uncertain hope.

We reached Pomona at dusk. The tie yard there was getting ready to close. The buyer casually looked over the load while my heart was bouncing against the roof of my mouth. It seemed like he looked for an eternity, but I'm sure now it was about 15 seconds before he made his pronouncement.

He deposited a wad of tobacco juice before he spoke, "Fellow, we can't use them, they're all seconds." The hangman's trap had finally sprung!

As I dangled there, I managed to plead, "Mister, I gotta sell these. Won't you give me anything for them?" He started to walk away, but my last plea must have awakened some compassion from deep within his bosom, and he said, "Fella, I guess I can use them for corner posts. I'll pay you five dollars for the load."

Noah and I dumped the ties, the buyer wrote me a check for five dollars, and I turned to Noah and asked him what I owed him. Noah coughed a bit like he was embarrassed and started kind of calculating, "Well, Dick, I brought my truck over early this morning from Brandsville — that's 6 miles—helped you load the ties and drove to West Plains — that's another 13 miles, and then to Pomona and helped you unload — that's another 12 miles. Counting the gas and use of the truck and everything," he said sort of apologetically, "I'll have to charge you five dollars just to break even."

No doubt, Noah had fulfilled his part of the contract. I silently endorsed the check for five dollars and handed it to Noah to fulfill my part of the contract. Then I climbed into the truck and we started the rattling, freezing trip on the road back to West Plains. Neither of us spoke a word. It was dark when we started back. The streets were empty when we drove onto the square in West Plains. Instead of heading out East Main Street for home, without a word of explanation Noah pulled three quarters of the way around the square and started down Washington Avenue. He stopped and parked in front of Bob Samuelson's liquor store and got out without a word. He was gone for a short time and came out with a pint of whiskey that was labeled "Two Naturals." Still without a word, he unscrewed the cap and handed it to me. Without a word I took it and swallowed two large drinks of liquid fire and handed it back to the silent Noah and he took a long drink. Not a word was exchanged.

Noah drove me to our house. By that time the whiskey was dulling quite a bit of the disappointment of the day. I stepped from the bitter cold into the warmth of the King heater. The whiskey, combined with the warmth of the wood fire, began to have its salubrious effect on my spirit.

Doc was waiting in eager expectation. "What did we get?" he exclaimed as he rose to meet me. I began recounting the sad experiences of the day. He seemed incredulous until he caught the strong odor of whiskey mingled with the explanation of sad experiences. I could see his expression turn from incredulity to disgust. "You spent our money on whiskey!" he accused. No matter how hard I tried to convince him otherwise, the strong odor of the liquor spoke more eloquently than my words, and Doc stomped up to his loft to bed.

The next day he approached the matter more philosophically, and though he never really acted like he completely disbelieved me, I always felt that he never did fully accept my explanation.

Doc stayed with us until I left in '38. He moved up near his daughters in Willow Springs, about 20 miles away. After I came back from service in '46, I received a post card from him describing the way to his house. Somehow I got too busy and never got around to visiting him before he passed away.

In 1948, I formed the National Guard Company, which had been mobilized into the federal army in 1939. The Company was reformed into a Heavy Weapons Company and was comprised of a mix of WW II veterans and young recruits. Our summer encampment was at Fort Leonard Wood, and some of the new recruits stood rather in awe of the veterans. One of the vets was John Kirk who was a prisoner of the Japanese during the war, having been taken prisoner on Wake Island, and another was Henry Hayes who went through the Battle of the Bulge, and a number of others. The young recruits kept asking some of the veterans what some of their worst experiences were. I remember John Kirk telling about the Japanese taking a bunch of the prisoners to Shanghai and giving details of their terrible treatment. A number of the others related some of their worst experiences. One night at a session, several of them asked me what I considered my worst experience.

Now I had enlisted in the service at the start of the war. I had been in a group of four Marine fighter squadrons used by the Navy as guinea pigs to see if the Corsair, the Navy's fastest fighter, could be landed on the deck of the slow Jeep Carriers. Yet I brushed aside all my experiences of the war and replied without hesitation, "Back in the winter of '36-'37 I helped a fellow hack a load of post oak logs into ties with a broadax."

McGinnis

McGINNIS WAS DIFFERENT SOMEHOW. He was a rather small fellow, five feet eight inches or so, and he had a slender build. His hair was dark brown, almost black, with just a glint of red. You've seen hair like that, haven't you? It's real dark brown in which, when the sun hits it a certain way, one sees a slight shimmer of red. His eyes were as dark as his hair, maybe darker. They were intense eyes, serious eyes without much laughter in them, and they were set in a fine-featured, almost delicate, rather narrow face.

You wouldn't have noticed him in a crowd. He was quiet and reserved, and there was nothing about him to draw your attention. Even when you were around him with just two or three other fellows, it was easy to overlook him. It wasn't that he was unfriendly or anything like that. Whenever you spoke to him, he responded with a soft, pleasant voice, but it was always in a serious way. It's hard to explain. He was generally pleasant, but he was *always* serious.

Come to think of it, looking back, I can never remember him smiling. I suppose he did. He was bound to have smiled sometimes, but this is something I don't remember about him. I can't remember seeing him drink a beer or a highball either. Perhaps he did on occasion; I just don't ever remember seeing him do it. He wouldn't have drunk it with you, you understand; he would have quietly drunk it at the bar alone, and you wouldn't have even noticed.

I never saw him with a girl. He may have had one back in his hometown, but if he did, he never mentioned her. And while nearly everyone had some girl's picture on their dresser or some place, Mac was the exception. The only thing Mac kept on his dresser was a model of that forked-winged Corsair that he had made himself. It was a beautiful piece of work, and he had spent hours projecting and perfecting each detail. Everything was to scale. From the dihedral of the inverted gull wing to the hook on the arresting gear, each part was an identical replica of the real thing. He painted it sea blue and hand-rubbed the finish. It even had real rubber on the wheels.

I hadn't known Mac before going to Pollocksville. A number of us were transferred from SBD squadrons to three new Corsair squadrons being formed around Cherry Point, and I drew the one at Pollocksville. The Corps was small enough then that you had at least a casual acquaintance with most of the other pilots. You had either seen them or met them at some other base, but I didn't remember having ever seen Mac before.

Pollocksville was built in an isolated spot just a few miles from the swamps and consisted of a single landing strip, a small squadron building, a hangar and a few barracks. Most of the married officers lived in New Bern, and commuted to the base every day. There was no recreation on the base. The government was on a crash program to get three fighter squadrons ready for the Pacific theatre as quickly as possible, so if you were a pilot you flew or played ping pong or acey ducey while you waited to fly — everyone but Mac, that is. When he wasn't flying, he was out around the planes, either at the hangar or the apron. Sometimes he would come into the ready room and find a chair in a corner and study navigation, or the Corsair Specification Manual, or some manual on armament; but generally he'd be out examining the planes, watching the flights, the landings, and just everything he could see or find out about that plane.

I remember the first time I saw him. I had ridden to the base with Wiley. We both were married and lived in New Bern. We drove up to the squadron building and reported for duty; then I went out to look over the planes. I had never flown the Corsair before and wanted to look it over. It was there that I saw Mac.

He was standing in front of a plane, just two or three feet from the big three-bladed prop, and was gazing at that two-thousand horsepower engine with a look of rapture and awe. He took a step forward and softly touched the prop, then ran his hand up and down one of the blades as if he were caressing it. After that he walked slowly around the plane feeling the fuselage, the wings and the tail section, until he came around to the engine again. I walked over and introduced myself. He barely took his eyes off the plane to acknowledge my introduction and to give me his name. He didn't act curt or unfriendly, just detached. His concentration was solely on that plane.

We were assigned to the same division. He flew

wing on Wiley who was the division leader. I led the second section, and Turnbull, a big half Indian from Oklahoma, was my wingman. While you might overlook Mac on the ground, when he crawled into that plane and took that bird into the air, he would get your attention. It seemed as if his true personality didn't project itself until he crawled into a cockpit. While on the ground he was quiet and reserved; once he was airborne he became assertive, outgoing and critical as the devil of anyone who didn't measure up to his standard of flying.

I learned that he hadn't flown a Corsair before he came to Pollocksville, but within a week he knew more about that plane than anyone in the squadron, including the mechanic and the major. It was rather irritating at first. If he saw you make a sloppy landing or a bad approach, he'd tell you what you were doing wrong just like he was your instructor.

I remember the first time I took a Corsair up on a familiarization flight, and I was playing around to see what it would do. I dropped the nose, shoved the throttle forward and hauled the stick back to do a loop. I was used to that sluggish SBD, but this bird responded quick as a cat and pulled so many g's on me I blacked out like I was inside a jug. I didn't lose consciousness, but my sight was completely gone. I shoved the stick as far forward as I could, cranking the trim tab at the same time. I was trying to throw some negative g's so my sight would return. I know it was only for a few seconds, but it seemed as if I hung there for half an hour before the plane began wallowing forward from a near vertical position, and I could see again.

I was trying to put myself together to give it another try, when a crisp voice barked out over the UHF, "Next time don't horse back on the stick so hard, Doc. You aren't flying a Turkey!" At that moment Mac flew up on my right wing.

Well, I knew I had horsed back on the stick too hard. He didn't have to tell me. I wasn't in flight school anymore, and he wasn't my instructor. Of course, he *was* right. I had horsed the stick back too hard, but somehow it pricked a person's pride to have one's mistakes so bluntly pointed out to you by someone of your own rank with no more experience than you had.

Within a couple of months though, everyone seemed to pay attention to anything Mac pointed out. I guess we all recognized he was dead serious about this flying, and anything he told us he really meant for your own good. Most of the time he was right, too. That made the big difference.

Oh, once in a while someone was rubbed the wrong way. There was the time Lebo and Mac got in a dogfight. Lebo was a big muscular fellow from Georgia. He was a cop in some small Georgia town before the war. He had a rather low boiling point. He was a good pilot and was nervy on the ground or in the air. On one training flight our division was supposed to attack Lebo's division. The sky was full of thunderheads that day, and we were weaving in and out of them trying to spot Lebo's division. Wiley saw them first, about two thousand feet below us. Following Wiley's lead, all four planes in the division rolled over and attacked Lebo's planes.

They hadn't spotted us before we streaked past them, but once they did, we all broke up into individual dogfights with the other division. Mac had drawn Lebo, and they were dodging through the clouds, climbing, diving, scissoring, each trying to get the advantage. I guess it looked as if it was going to be a draw when Lebo went through a cloud and did a 180 in the cloud. Mac couldn't see what Lebo was doing, so he climbed about a thousand feet and was trying to find him. Lebo turned back when he got out of the cloud, and saw he was behind and below Mac. He was trying to climb in behind Mac and get on his tail when Mac rolled over, saw Lebo and dove his plane straight at Lebo's. If Lebo hadn't turned away, the pieces would still be falling out of the Carolina sky. At the last split second Lebo rolled to the right, and in a matter of seconds Mac was locked in on his tail. Believe me, when Mac locked in on your tail, you might as well figure on company until he said goodbye.

Well, Lebo was waiting for Mac when he came into the ready room. He was at his boiling point and had spilled over. When Mac walked in the door, Lebo stormed up to him with his face all red and yelled, "Listen here, you damned little squirt, the next time you pull a stunt like that, I'll ram the hell right out of you."

Lebo would have made two of Mac, and as he stood towering above Mac with his fists clutched and yelling down at him, it seemed such an unequal pairing as to appear ridiculous. But Mac never gave an inch. He looked up at Lebo with those dark, serious eyes; and just as relaxed as you'd ever want to see, he spoke in his calm, soft voice, "Lebo, you just do what you think you have to do." He paused and then added, "And you can be dead sure I will."

You know, after that Lebo calmed down and always seemed to go out of his way to be nice to Mac. He'd talk to him about different tactics, and they just got along fine.

Our squadron commander was Major Spinks. He was rather pudgy, with a round face, and his eyes bugged out a bit. He was an E base instructor before he received a squadron command, and he had only flown the Corsair once or twice before he took the command. He led a division, but his division didn't fly as much as the rest of us, for Spinks took the paperwork seriously. In fact, it was my impression he preferred it to flying, but ever so often he'd lead his division on a training flight. When they came in, he'd always give them a critique and explain to them what they were doing wrong.

We all had to take turns flying the tow plane for gunnery practice. We'd pull a big sleeve a hundred yards or so behind the tow plane, and the division practicing would get above it and make runs on it, firing their .50 calibre machine guns at it. Each man's ammunition was a different color on the bullets, and if you hit the sleeve, the bullet would leave a little bit of that color. That way you could tell who was hitting the target and who wasn't.

One day Mac had to fly the tow plane when Spinks took his division up for gunnery practice. I guess it became a bit boring for him flying that tow plane straight and level, for the fellows in Spinks' division said Mac would call out every time they made a run and tell them what they were doing wrong. He did that two or three times with Spinks, too, and about the third time Spinks told him to stay off the air.

When they got down, Mac went over where they were examining the sleeve and counting their hits. The major had three or four, and that was about what the other three had. Mac remarked softly, but with the authority of one who knew what he was talking about, "You all got too far behind your target before starting your run. That way you got sucked back and didn't hit much. You should have that sleeve looking like a sieve."

Well, he had said similar things to everyone who flew with him, and most of us started to pay attention, for Mac was the best shot in the squadron. Spinks had never flown with him though and didn't know how good he was. Also, he had been an instructor at an E base where cadets didn't point out what the instructor did wrong. To have a junior officer critique him didn't set too well. They said his eyes bugged out a little more than usual. He glared at Mac, then stalked off without saying a word. A stronger man would have welcomed constructive criticism, and it wouldn't have bothered him, but Spinks was an insecure person. All Mac's advice did for him was to bruise his vanity and threaten him. It didn't bother Mac though. He just called it as he saw it. He wasn't pushing for promotion or self-acclaim, just proficiency.

The next day Spinks scheduled his division for gunnery again. Loval was Spinks' wing man, but on the flight schedule for this gunnery practice, it showed McGinnis' name instead of Loval. They said Mac didn't give a word of advice to anyone the entire flight, which was unusual for him. He'd be on Spinks' wing when Spinks made his run, but he wouldn't follow him. Instead, he'd pour on the gas and get farther ahead of the target and higher before he started his run. The second section followed Mac's lead instead of Spinks. When they landed and counted their hits, Spinks had his usual three or four. The boys in the second section each had twenty-some odd, but Mac had over a hundred when they stopped counting.

Spinks didn't say a word this time either, but they could tell he was smarting. He turned, walked away, and never flew with Mac again. In fact, it seemed to me that Spinks studiously ignored him. If it bothered Mac, you couldn't tell it. He flew every chance he got, and if you flew with him and turned in a sloppy flight, he'd let you know. I believe he looked upon the squadron as *his* squadron, not for the sake of position, understand, but just because he was part of it. He wanted it to be the best squadron in the Corps. That's why he prodded you if you began to slack off. You were on his team, and he wanted his team to be the best. He didn't ask any more of you than he did of himself.

We went by troop train to Mojave — from the sticky, humid weather of Carolina to the dry bleak weather of the desert. It was there we learned we were going to be assigned to an aircraft carrier instead of land-based. Our training became more intensive. They slung rocket racks on our Corsairs. In addition to our six .50 calibre machine guns, we now carried three five-inch rockets under each wing, and sometimes the big 1450-lb. "Tiny Tim" rocket. We were to be the first to use the "Tiny Tim." It was our division that made the best scores on all the rocket runs, and we had that special camaraderie that comes to individuals who throw all their skills and efforts together to accomplish a common goal. Mac was buoyant. It was a serious buoyancy, if you know what I mean. He didn't laugh and cut up or anything like that. I guess you'd say he was in a state of serious exhilaration. I know it's contradictory, but that's the closest way I can describe how he was.

He never missed a chance to fly, and one morning he was down at the hangar when one of the mechanics asked him if he wanted to test fly one of the planes which just had an engine overhaul. Of course, Mac was ready. He took it up and was putting it through the paces when he spotted an army boy flying a P-51. Mac couldn't resist jumping him. The army boy jumped right back, and they flew all over the sky in a dogfight, each trying to get on the other's tail. The P-51 wasn't cluttered with all those rocket racks, so it was cleaner and had the acceleration edge, but Mac was making up for that in finesse. Finally, Mac got on his tail and the P-51 pulled up into a chandelle. When the P-51 rolled out, he was just a little above his stalling speed. Mac, in the heavier Corsair, was right on his tail, but when he rolled out, he was too slow and his plane stalled and went into a spin.

The Corsair had a flat spin, and if it got around on you two or three times, it could be wicked. You had to get the opposite rudder and the stick full forward and hold them there to bring it out. That took muscle, not finesse. If you let that stick back just an inch, you wouldn't have much luck. I've known fellows who would shove one foot on the opposite rudder and jam the stick forward with the other foot. Even then you had to shove with all your might to hold it full forward. Mac was a small man, and though he was wiry, I guess he didn't have the strength to keep the stick forward. At least, he didn't bring it out of the spin, and that's what I would judge was the problem. At any rate, he rode it down for about ten thousand feet trying to bring it out. About two thousand feet from the deck he forced his hood open, unfastened his safety belt and the centrifugal force flung him clear of the plane to the outside. The tail almost clipped him as it swung around, and he was afraid to pull his rip cord for fear the tail would snag it. Finally, about seven hundred feet from the deck he pulled the cord and just made two or three oscillations before he hit. The plane crashed slightly ahead of him. We saw the smoke from the field, and the meat wagon drove out in the brush and picked him up.

Mac was all right. They sent him up to sick bay to check him out, but he was back in the squadron room in a couple of hours explaining to those who gathered around just what had happened. Swenson, the flight officer, brought out the accident report forms and told him to fill them out. Everyone was joking and kidding him in that bizarre way men who live close to death do to those they like and respect.

When Mac finished filling out the accident report, he took it to Swenson, and then Swenson took it to Major Spinks. A little bit later Swenson came out and told Mac the major wanted to see him. The major's office was adjacent to the ready room, and Mac hadn't more than stepped in the door before the major starting bawling him out. He called Mac an incompetent showoff, and told him any man who couldn't bring a plane out of a spin should be in the infantry. He went on and on degrading Mac for about fifteen or twenty minutes. You would have thought Mac had lost the war. Then, without giving Mac a chance to say a word, he told him to get out.

Mac's eyes were glistening when he left the major's office, and he immediately left the ready room and went outside. Wiley and I, Turnbull and most of the other fellows followed him to give him our support. We had lost several planes before, and the major hadn't said a peep. Mac thanked us and walked up to the barracks to his room. The next day the major cut Mac from the squadron.

We couldn't believe our eyes when we saw it on the bulletin board. A pall went over the whole squadron. When Mac came in and read it, he looked as if he had been shot. He turned straight on his heel and went to the barracks without a word. We found him there sitting at his desk running his fingers over that beautiful model of a Corsair he had made. He was assigned to a pilot's pool in San Diego and given a week's leave.

He didn't take his leave, but stayed in his room for several days. About the fourth day he started going around the hangar again. Even though he was supposed to be in San Diego in three days, he didn't pack his things or seem to be in a hurry to get squared away. Several of us would drop in to see him every evening, but he wasn't the same. You could tell his pride had been cut to the quick. It was the morning of the sixth day, the day before he was supposed to leave for San Diego, that Mac went down to the hangar and asked the chief mechanic if he had any planes he needed tested. Of course, he did. Mac took one of those birds up and put it through its paces not too far from the field. It was a beautiful exhibition of flying. He did every maneuver in the book and added a few of his own. Then he put that Corsair into a spin and rode it into the ground. This time he didn't bail out.

Bolen had seen the whole thing, and he caught up with Wiley and me to give us the news as we were starting for the ready room. We drove to the ready room

and went directly to the major's office. He was sitting behind his desk drinking a coke, and going over some papers. He looked up at us inquiringly with those bug eyes of his and Wiley said, "Major, McGinnis just spun in."

The major didn't even blink those bug eyes. "The hell he did," he said. "Say, tell Swenson to bring me the flight schedules. We're leaving for Santa Barbara in three days."

Bart

BART WAS PLEASANTLY SURPRISED. The train was not very crowded, so he picked an empty seat and sat down by the window. He tried to sort out his feelings. It was as though a thick blanket of anxiety, which had enveloped him for so long, had started to evaporate. The war was over and he was headed home to Ruth.

They had married just after he had been commissioned three years ago. They had grown up in the same town, had gone to high school together, and had known each other for years prior to their graduation. They were engaged before the outbreak of the war, but when it became evident that the United States was going to enter the war and Bart decided to become a Naval aviator, they put off the marriage until he received his commission. The day after he received his wings and became a Marine Corps officer, they were married.

They were able to spend a number of months together while he went through further training and was assigned to a fighter squadron. It was a happy time filled with the comradeship they developed with the other young married couples and with the single fellows in the squadron, and the almost exhilarating, carefree atmosphere that people use as a screen to separate their present lives from the uncertainty of realizing that tomorrow could be cataclysmic. You squeezed all the happiness you could out of every day. Even little quarrels seemed as though they added instead of detracted from the memories.

He could close his eyes and smell the fragrance of her hair, see the blue of her eyes and how they twinkled in such a mischievous way when she would tease him about some little thing. Then, just as he would be basking in those pleasant memories, Miller's face would suddenly surface in his memories, and he would be smothered again with an overwhelming gush of sorrow, sadness and, worst of all, guilt. In anguish, he would relive the events all over again.

He had known Miller from his cadet days. Their first meeting was at St. Mary's in California. Miller was from a little town in Kansas. He had dark wavy hair and brown eyes, and he was well built, about 6'1" in height, quiet, well-mannered and well liked. They both received their wings and commission in the Corps at Corpus Christi the same day. Within a week they parted ways. Bart was assigned to a fighter squadron on the East Coast. He didn't know at the time where Miller was sent.

Bart stayed on the East coast almost a year. Ruth joined him and they roomed in a boarding house with a couple of other young fliers and their wives. It was a joyous time. None of them had a car, and the fellows had to hitch-hike each morning to the base and bum a ride back to town at night, but everyone shared at that time, and there were no problems. Even the inconveniences seemed pleasant.

Bart and Ruth formed close friendship with other married couples in the squadron. As the first Marine fighters to participate in the European theater, Bart's squadron was slated to be shipped out to participate in the D-Day invasion, but word leaked out. It became the talk of the town, so the brass canceled it, and instead the squadron was sent to the West coast where they started training for carrier duty.

Bart was cautious by nature, and he was in an outfit where caution in itself could be dangerous. For instance, they were hanging six 5-inch rockets under the wings, in addition to tip tanks and a couple of bombs; that, with a load of .50 caliber ammo for the six wing guns, pushed the gross weight past eight tons when you were all fueled up. You had to firewall that 2000-horsepower engine to get your speed up. Bart was inclined to nurse his engine, and as a result had a tendency to fall behind in exercises when flying with his division. He had a bit of trouble with his carrier landings, too. The squadron was assigned a CVE, a small carrier ship that couldn't make over seven knots, and if you didn't have much wind over the deck to help slow you down, the landings could be a bit hairy.

The squadron had to be downsized for carrier duty, and Bart was cut from the squadron. Bart was convinced it was because the Major didn't like him. After being together for over a year of intensive training, the squadron had become almost like family to Bart. When he read the bulletin board and saw he had been cut from the squadron, he felt sick and empty all over. Ruth went home to Oregon, and Bart was shipped to a pilot's pool in Hawaii.

Bart hadn't been the only pilot cut from the squadron; Smalley was, too. Smalley just didn't like the idea of landing on a jeep carrier. He stayed with the squadron though while they prepared, went to El Centro and practiced field carrier landings, but when the squadron went aboard ship for a shake-down cruise, he decided against it. He took too many wave-offs and was cut. Smalley was sent to the same pool in Hawaii as Bart. Smalley was a rather large Indian from Oklahoma. He was married to a part Indian girl from his hometown. He would have liked to stay in the squadron too, but his dislike of flying off of a jeep carrier had the greater weight, so he deliberately cut himself out by taking too many wave-offs. He sent his wife back to Oklahoma with their baby girl, and unlike Bart, Smalley rather looked forward to the next venture life had in store for him.

They boarded a cruiser in San Diego the middle of February, and within a week were in Hawaii. They reported in to the Marine base at Eva, were assigned quarters, and met some old friends from their training days. There were a number of pilots in the pool and an equal number of rumors. Every way you turned there was a different rumor as to where they were being sent. From time to time some were sent as replacement pilots to various squadrons, but there was the persistent scuttlebutt that squadrons were going to be formed for some invasion duty, perhaps the main islands of Japan proper. The weather was so lovely and the odor of pineapple permeating the air so delightful that Bart's spirits began to revive. Besides, Smalley was a big help. He was the type of fellow who rode the thermal currents of life like a sea gull soaring. Smalley's easy-going attitude of taking the events of life in stride as they came was infectious, and Bart began to get a nagging hope that they might just get to fight the rest of the war in this paradise; if only Ruth were with him, it would be perfect.

The first week of March the rumors began to jell. Word was definite that Okinawa was going to be invaded, and a few days later both Smalley and Bart were assigned to a squadron that was slated to be a part of the invasion forces. They didn't go with the first group, but during the first week in April they and several other pilots boarded a small carrier that was ferrying planes to the battle site. On the evening of the 4th they anchored off Higashi beach, where the Marines had first landed.

The invasion fleet stretched as far as the eye could see. Bart was amazed, and the word was it exceeded the invasion fleet that took place in Europe on D-Day. There was every conceivable type of vessel you could imagine. It didn't appear to Bart like there was much order to the way they were anchored. The report was that there was little resistance to the landing of the troops, and this created an optimistic hope that this campaign would not be the bloody affair that categorized previous battles with the Japanese. At any rate, Bart knew that the enemy air power had been badly crippled, and they had lost most of their carriers. Perhaps this battle would be a piece of cake and they'd be out of here in no time at all. These were contagious thoughts, and Bart even began to think of going home. When he closed his eyes and let his mind drift to the happy times, the war could seem far away, almost unreal, even though there was the hustle and scurrying about of people around you. He was jarred out of these idyllic thoughts when a squall hit. Although he hadn't been very observant of the weather at the time, it seemed to Bart as if it came out of nowhere. One minute the sun was shining, the next minute there was a gale and the rain came pouring down. Everyone scattered below deck to wait it out. Besides Smalley and Bart, there were six other pilots waiting to go ashore. They received word in the evening to have their gear ready for transportation to their base the first thing in the morning.

They were all reporting to the same squadron, so the next morning immediately after breakfast mess eight young pilots were on deck, suppressing their nervous anticipation with an assumed nonchalance and light banter. The sky was partially obscured by low cumulus clouds. Every imaginable type of ocean-going vessel was there. The beach was a beehive of activity, with all types of supplies arriving and being unloaded. To the north came the sounds of battle, shells exploding, the familiar whistling sound that told them Corsairs were giving ground support to the troops. Bart wondered silently how the pilots could see to support troops with the clouds so low and the visibility so poor. Occasionally ships' anti aircraft guns would add their high-pitched staccato, and the deep belch of a battleship's big guns would be followed by a ripple of some of the shock waves passing over.

And they waited. It was always the waits that were exasperating. No matter what was taking place you could be sure it involved waiting. Around 13:00 a small landing craft pulled alongside the carrier and a marine corporal came aboard. He announced himself as

Corporal Cooksie of the 3rd Marine Amphibious Corps, read off the names of the pilots waiting and told them he was to escort them to their base. They all got their gear and climbed aboard the landing craft, which was being operated by a navy seaman. The corporal was slim, sandy-headed, confident and friendly. Cooksie was obviously happy to be transporting the pilots to their new home, rather than being in the line. He also was as full of the news, rumors and guesses as a radio commentator, and he dispensed it with just as much assurance and abandon.

The 3rd Marine Amphibious Corps was in a mopping-up campaign for the north part of the island. The XXIV Corps of the Tenth Army had run into the defensive fortifications of the Japanese in the southern part and they were tough; that was where the fighting was going to be; word was that the Kamikazes were coming. The weather was stinking. It got awfully muddy when it rained. The Japs had the natives thinking the Americans would torture them and rape their women; when they found out that they would be treated well, they were becoming friendly. Some of the pilots were already getting the Okinawa women to clean their tents, and the women were stealing their toilet paper. It seems that the women didn't know what it was for at first, and when they learned of its magical properties, they would swipe it from the tents they were cleaning. The Marines had secured two airstrips, and some Marine Corsairs were already supporting troops. The squadrons weren't full up yet; the rations were pretty good and were plentiful; Corporal Cooksie knew where you could get cold beer. In between his dispensing of information, he was collecting some from the fellows.

What outfits were they from, where they were from in the States, what they flew and whatever other information he could think of. It was obvious Cooksie was a main depository and dispenser of scuttlebutt, which made him an indispensable man of stature among his peers. Bart made a mental note to keep in contact with Cooksie.

The beach was a jumble of organized confusion. Landing craft of every kind and description were unloading supplies, which ranged from field rations to tanks. As fast as one vessel unloaded, another took its place. The seaman in charge of their mission steered expertly into a vacant slot, and the men unloaded their gear on the beach. All around them landing vessels were being unloaded. Some troops were still being landed. There was the usual shouting of orders, the cursing, grumbling, grunting of a great number of men doing hundreds of different tasks to accomplish a single objective, destroying the Japanese army holding the island. The landing craft immediately left for other duties. Cooksie told the pilots to stay by their gear until he brought up their transportation. He left and was gone but a short time before he came driving up in a carryall.

They all loaded into the carryall, and after about an hour of bouncing over rough roads arrived at the airstrip. It had been taken over from the Japanese just a short time ago, and some of the Japanese structures were in use. There was a hangar and a pilot's ready room at one end of the strip, and a short distance from the ready room, adjacent to it were a couple of sections of tents which housed the personnel. The Corsairs were parked along the side across from the ready room.

Everyone was busy at some task, planes were being loaded with armament of various types, and some were landing and taking off after being rearmed.

The airstrip was narrow; having been built to accommodate the lighter Japanese planes, and construction had already begun to widen it. There was evidence of recently repaired bomb craters. Quite a bit of dust was over everything, and the weather was cool. Later when the rains started Bart would long for the dust. Smalley and Bart were assigned to tent #3. Each tent would accommodate four pilots, and they took their gear there. Their two other tent mates were gone, and after putting their gear in place, they proceeded to headquarters to report in. Headquarters was in the ready room. It was there Bart discovered one of his tent mates would be his old acquaintance from cadet days, R.J. Miller. The other was a flyer by the name of Lewis. Neither Bart nor Smalley knew him. The duty roster showed that both men were flying and were due back in about an hour.

They met Captain Seitz, the executive officer. He was already acquainted with their flight jackets and had gone over their logbooks. Seitz was pleasant in sort of a serious way; he told them they would team with Miller and Lewis to form a division and that Miller would be the division leader. Bart would fly wing on Miller in the first section, and Smalley would fly wing on Lewis who would be leading the second section. He told them they were short on aircraft and would fly what was available and that they would be on the flight roster the next day. After giving them that information, he looked from one to the other and asked, "Any questions?" When both replied in the negative, he added, "If you're short any supplies, see the supply sergeant." The interview was over, and they went back to the tent.

It was almost twilight when they heard the planes land, and a half hour later after the debriefing Lewis and Miller showed up at the tent. Both men showed the weariness that comes after you land and relax from the tension of several hours of strenuous concentration. Introductions were exchanged all around. Lewis was a rather stocky, blond-haired fellow from Georgia who had been a small town policeman prior to the war. He was single and engaged to a girl from his hometown. It had been two years since he had been back to the States. Smalley and he hit it off well and within fifteen minutes were sharing tidbits of information as if they had been acquainted for years. Bart and Miller greeted each other warmly. The memory of their cadet days quickly wrapped them in a blanket of camaraderie, and they had several years of catching up to do.

They were both surprised to learn that they had been stationed very close to each other several different times, but somehow or other had never had occasion to see each other. Miller had been stationed at Cherry Point when Bart was at Pollicksville. Both had lived in New Bern. When Miller was at Santa Barbara, Bart was at Mojave, and so it went. Miller had married the widow of a friend of his who had been killed in a crash at Mojave. His wife's name was Ann, and he had her picture displayed on his footlocker, a pretty girl with auburn hair and hazel eyes. They had been married almost two years. When Miller was shipped overseas, Ann went back to her parent's home in New Mexico to give birth to a little girl that Miller had never seen. Miller carried the picture of the baby in his wallet, which he proudly displayed to Bart.

Bart, in turn, took the picture of his blue-eyed, blond-haired Ruth from his footlocker for Miller to see. After getting acquainted and filling each other in on their families, Smalley and Bart were anxious to get all of the information possible on what to expect from their flying duties, which was to start promptly the next day.

Miller gave them the rundown on what to expect. Seitz had briefed them on their two new teammates right after they landed and reported in.

"I'll lead the division, and Lewis will be the second section leader. Bart will fly my wing and Smalley will be Lewis' wingman. We're going to be flying close support to the ground troops. We'll be using napalm, rockets and our .50s for strafing. The Japs are holed up in caves on the south part of the island, and it looks as if it will take a while to root them out. The spotters will let us know what targets they want us to take out. Some of the caves are damned hard to find from the air as they're well camouflaged. We'll make individual runs, and some of the time I'll be the spotter. I'll fly down and size up the target, and then the three of you will individually hit it. If any of you see that it's all clear, you can signal that and we'll chase another rabbit. Now some of those caves are fairly low in the hills where they're located, and when you fling napalm in you're going to have to watch that you don't follow it in. One or two have made that mistake. Keep your eyes open for Jap planes; we keep hearing the Kamikazes are coming. They played hell last month with the Ben Franklin. Incidentally, watch out for Japs around your area, too. This part is pretty well secure, but they've had to shoot a couple or three at the other base. Keep your eyes open. When the Kamikazes come, we'll have to start flying combat patrols along with troop support."

Lewis interjected some of his observations. "The weather can be stinky, and it's never ideal. When it gets real soupy, it's good to snuggle close and depend on who is leading to do the navigating to the target. Otherwise, it's pretty easy to get separated and miss the target that's spotted."

After some additional information was exchanged, they all went to their bunks, and Bart finally drifted off into the restless sleep that he had experienced so many times in the past three years. He was wide awake at the first sound of reveille. Miller was already dressed, had been to the head and shaved. Lewis was in the head. Smalley was getting dressed. Miller told them that he and Lewis would wait for them to get dressed and they would all go to breakfast mess together where they would meet some other members of their squadron.

The mess tent was set back from the circle of tents housing the pilots, was about three times larger, and had benches around the tables where the men ate. They picked up their trays and joined the mess line, filled their trays with the familiar scrambled eggs, fried spam, toast, etc. Lewis and Miller introduced them to the fellows at their table, and they listened to the chatter and speculation about their missions of the day.

After breakfast they reported to the ready room. It was just breaking daylight. They were introduced to the twelve or so other pilots by Seitz and met Major Brooks who commanded the squadron.

With Brooks there was no small talk. Before a large detailed map of Okinawa he outlined what were the targets of the day. The Japanese had chosen to defend the southern part of the island. The area was rugged and honeycombed with caves, making it extremely difficult to get tanks in position to help the infantrymen. Navy guns could just do so much, but couldn't pinpoint the help that was needed. The flame-thrower crews were exposed to withering fire getting close enough to operate, and so napalm, rockets and strafing seemed to be the most effective help. Each division would have a two-hour mission, and then would come back to the base, rearm and refuel. It would be the responsibility of each division leader to make sure each pilot inspected the armament they were carrying to see that it was properly loaded and armed. If they ran out of armament sooner, the division leader would bring the flight back for rearming. The pilots would be flying close support to the ground crews, and it was important to keep a sharp eye on where the troops were at all times. They had to get close enough to do some good, but to always make certain they were ahead of the troops.

Brooks added that they had received word that the Kamikazes were coming from Kyushus. If Kamikazes came, combat patrols would start on a round-the-clock basis in addition to the close support. He told them to keep their eyes open for Japanese around the base as the area wasn't totally secure, and to watch at all times for Japanese planes. Brooks was leading and spotting for the first division, and they took off immediately after the morning's briefing.

Miller and Lewis helped Smalley and Bart check their armament and went over the firing procedure with them. Then approximately an hour after Brook's division left, they were in the air. The distance from their base to the target area was such a short distance that they were upon it immediately after joining up. Visibility was poor. Patches of low cumulus clouds kept drifting over the target area, and the division circled for about ten minutes before Miller signaled he was going down to spot the target. When he peeled off, Bart strained his eyes to follow him, and when he saw a flash of fire from a bursting napalm bomb, he started his dive. It was over almost before he had time to think. He hadn't realized just how nervous he had been. The knot in his stomach just wouldn't go away. They were trying to flush out a good-sized group of Japanese from a cave on the reverse slope of a hill. Mortar and artillery fire from the cave and others like it were making the infantry advance slow going and costly. The Japanese were tenacious and fearless fighters, and it seemed as if the ground had to be taken one foot at a time.

On the first run Bart was nervous and neglected to flip on his selector switch; the second one the napalm bomb he released didn't go near enough to do any good, and he resolved to do better with his rockets. Before he hardly realized, it was time to return for rearming.

Miller was tactful in his criticism, but he carefully explained to Bart that to be effective with the napalm he had to get closer to the target before his release. He didn't mention Bart's dry run, but sensed Bart was embarrassed enough so there was no need to. By the end of the day and several flights behind him, the knot in Bart's stomach had been replaced by hunger and fatigue. They had been in the air eight hours, and Bart had quickly adapted to the tactics.

Bart

The next day the Kamikazes struck the Hagushi anchorage, downing twenty-two ships ranging from destroyers to mine vessels. Fortunately, no large vessels were struck, and from that day forward Bart's squadron went on combat air patrol as well as ground support. They started flying at the break of day and finished at dark. The weather didn't help matters. The dust turned to mud when the rains started. The mud seeped into everything, your shoes, your clothes, your cockpit, and even your hair. You took off and landed in torrential downpours.

Mechanics repaired engines in the rain. If you ran off the ramp, you were stuck in mud that stuck bulldozers. But still you flew, because the rains also brought the Kamikazes.

They were a brave lot, those Kamikazes. Most of them were poorly trained, and they flew anything that would get them off the ground, old bombers, fighters, observation planes, crates that would last for just one flight. Many of the pilots were in their teens, and they flew knowing that this one flight would be their last. But fly they did, and 3500 of them died in desperate individual attempts to save their country from invasion.

A Kamikaze could do terrible damage to a ship if it made a hit. Bart was well aware of what had happened to the Ben Franklin. He was a personal friend of some of the pilots aboard who had been killed, and the hundreds of ships in the Okinawa invasion force presented tempting targets to the Kamikaze.

After the sinking of the ships in Hagushi anchorage, the sailors in the hundreds of invasion ships would fire at any object flying, whether it was friend or foe.

One old salt expressed the sentiment succinctly when he said, "Shoot 'em all down and sort 'em out later."

The combination of bad weather and danger of being shot down by your own navy took all the glamour and picnic aura out of any portrait Bart had envisioned when he first started training. They flew from daylight to dark in weather that the birds sat out. If they weren't firing rockets or flinging napalm in hard-to-see caves right on the deck and then pulling up before they followed it in, they were flying combat patrol searching for the Kamikaze. Bart's old cautious habit of nursing his engine dissipated in the wringing, wrenching, grueling pace of flying they were being put through. They went to bed bone-weary and woke to repeat the same tasks the next day.

Besides, there was Miller, the quiet, steady, competent Miller, the division leader. You just couldn't let Miller down, for you always knew he would never let you down, and he was always considerate of his wingman. In the worst kind of weather you could fly on his wing and know he was looking out for the both of you. When the visibility was really bad, Bart would fly close enough on his wing to see him checking his chart board, and he always had a sense of confidence that Miller would bring them safely back to base.

When they were flying combat patrol, Miller would split the division and have each section fly a different vector. Lewis and Smalley would fly one vector and Miller and Bart another. It was in one of these instances that Miller received a call that a Kamikaze was approaching one of our carriers, and Miller and Bart turned to intercept. They were close to the end of their patrol and had expended most of their ammo. The Japanese was flying a Betty Bomber and had dived through the clouds at about 4500 feet when they spotted him about a half-mile away.

Miller, coming out of the clouds, fire-walled his plane and began firing his wing guns. Bart, behind Miller, was expecting Miller to break away when he had expended his ammunition. About this time, the ships below opened up their antiaircraft fire. Miller, out of ammo, dove his plane into the Jap with antiaircraft shells bursting all around him and chewed off the tail of the Japanese with that big Corsair propeller, causing the bomber to plunge into the ocean short of the ship it had targeted. When Miller pulled up, the targeted ship was still firing at him. It was fortunate their aim was so poor. Bart had followed Miller all the way, expecting Miller to break off when he ran out of ammo, so he ran into the ship's fire. He pulled up when Miller did, but not before he caught some of the bursting shrapnel in his starboard wing. He felt the shock and saw the jagged hole in the wing, but he could still control the plane, so he called Miller to throttle back. He eased up to Miller and Miller took them in.

The weather was stinking. When they landed, the rain was coming down in sheets; Bart was so close behind Miller that he landed in his slipstream. Instead of breaking off for the landing, Bart had just throttled back a bit and let Miller get in front. It always gave Bart a feeling of security to be flying close wing on Miller. He always knew he could depend on Miller looking after the both of them. In the foulest weather or the closest spots, Bart had that feeling of assurance.

If the Navy gunners were trigger-happy at the start of the Kamikaze attacks, after one hit the Enterprise in the middle of May, they became twice as bad. They would fire at our planes whether Japanese were in the area or not.

It was the last of May that a U.S. Cruiser shot down both Lewis and Smalley when they were returning from a combat patrol. Bart and Miller, on a separate vector, had landed 15 minutes earlier.

The cruiser got Lewis with a direct hit close to the cockpit and Lewis never got out. They struck Smalley's plane in the forward engine section, and Smalley was able to bail out. When he jumped, he pulled his ripcord before he was clear of his plane, and his chute caught on the tail of his aircraft and was pulling him with it. Smalley frantically was jerking the shrouds of the chute and was able to jerk it loose just in time to make one oscillation before he hit the water. The irony of the situation was that men from the same ship which shot him down pulled the cursing, mad Indian from Oklahoma out of the water.

A replacement named Shaw came in the next day to replace Lewis, and Smalley moved up to section leader.

Their flying kept alternating between troop support and combat patrol. As the Japanese gradually gave ground, they put more effort into their Kamikaze attacks from the air. Sometimes our men would get orders for one section to supply ground support while the other section went on patrol. It was all day flying whichever way it went, but on ground support you didn't face as much danger of being shot down by the Navy.

Miller's steady judgment and cool confidence was infectious, and the cautious uncertainty of Bart's nature began to be infused day by day by that steady judgment and cool confidence. Miller received his orders, and he proceeded deliberately to fulfill them with quiet confidence, no hesitation, no fanfare and no braggadocio. Flying day by day on his wing, Bart began to acquire those qualities.

There was something else that grew, too, along with his admiration, loyalty. Bart would have, without hesitation, followed Miller through the very gates of Hell itself. Miller had been very perceptive of Bart from the beginning. He immediately saw that Bart was unsure of himself, and Miller proceeded to build his confidence without calling attention to it. During the last two weeks when they had been flying as a single section, Miller, on occasion, had given Bart the lead and had assumed the wingman's position. He had even encouraged Bart on occasion to call the shots.

About a week after the Marines took Naha, intelligence received word that the Japanese were launching an all-out assault of Kamikaze from Kyushu. This was the third such report and, inasmuch as the previous two reports had not materialized, this one didn't create much of a stir. Miller split the division and sent Smalley and Shaw in one section on one vector and he took another. On this occasion he gave Bart the lead of his section.

The weather was poor, scattered cumulus at 3,000 ft., with solid monsoon-type clouds above. The rain was not heavy when they started out. They were almost 100 miles from base when the weather turned ugly, the rain started coming in torrents, and Bart turned back. It didn't improve on the way back. The ceiling dropped down to the deck, and Bart went solely on instruments. Miller, on his wing, was step down and flying so close he could almost have read Bart's instruments. Bart kept edging down to see if they could break out under the heavy layer of rain clouds. When the altimeter showed 100 feet and there was still no sign of a break and he couldn't see the deck, that old feeling of uncertainty began to engulf him. He took his eyes off the instruments and pulled his plot board to check their position. Out of the corner of his eye, he saw Miller hit the sea and instinctively pulled up and avoided that fate. He was horrified. He had flown his wingman into the ocean. Only the strong sense of self-preservation prevented him from deliberately diving his own plane in.

Mechanically, he gained altitude, somehow found the base and landed in a driving rain. He just sat there numb with grief and shock. He was jolted into action by the tower operator repeatedly asking him to clear the runway. He managed to follow the parking directions and continued to sit in the cockpit after he shut down his engine, until a line Sergeant jumped on the wing of his plane, tapped on his hood and asked him if he was all right. Then he crawled out of the plane, closed the hood and made his way to the ready room.

There were about 10 or 12 pilots who had just reported in, Seitz was there, and when Miller didn't land with him, he could tell they all suspected something had happened. Seitz asked him, and all Bart could say was that Miller had gone in. Seitz, recognizing that Bart was close to the breaking point, told him to go to his tent and write a report on the flight in the morning. He made a note of the time and conditions when Bart had landed.

When he reached his tent, he flung himself on the bunk without taking off his wet gear. He felt like he wanted to throw up. Smalley and Shaw came in, and the first thing Smalley did was ask Bart what had happened to Miller. All Bart could do was to stammer that he went in. He couldn't bring himself to tell Smalley the circumstances. Smalley knew the respect and admiration Bart had for Miller and could see that Bart was having emotional difficulty, so he didn't press him for details. When he went to the mess tent, he brought Bart back a hot cup of black coffee, set it beside his bunk and didn't query him further.

After an hour or so, Bart took off his wet gear and tried to sleep. He was so engulfed in sorrow and the feeling of guilt it was impossible to sleep, so he lay in his bunk, staring at the tent ceiling and dreading the morning when he would have to file his report.

Major Brooks read Bart's report carefully, asked him how he happened to be leading the section, and just nodded when Bart said Miller had requested it. Seitz told him he would fly with Smalley and Shaw, and a replacement for Miller would be arriving the next day. Smalley would lead the division and Bart the second section. The word had quickly spread that Miller had hit the ocean while flying wing on Bart, and none of the other pilots quizzed him about what had happened as they usually did when a pilot went in. Bart thought that they were talking about it out of his presence, and this enhanced his feeling of guilt and isolation.

A fellow by the name of Lott replaced Miller the next day, and Bart led the second section.

Smalley was his salvation. Easy-going, perceptive, Smalley began to draw him out of the depths of depression, just by including Bart in everything he did. He ate his meals with him, sought his advice on the missions, shared his mail with him, bragged on him every chance he got. Bart's depression gradually subsided to the point he began to make suggestions to Smalley on some aspects of their assignments.

About two weeks after Miller's death, Brooks called Bart in and handed him a letter from Miller's widow. She had written and asked for some of his comrades to give her the particulars of his death. Brooks gave the letter to Bart and asked that he write her. This almost threw him again, and Smalley helped him compose a letter and co-signed it with Bart. It was Smalley, the big, easy-going Indian from Oklahoma, who pulled Bart through.

It was easy to see the battle was winding down. Within a couple of weeks, the battle was over. Both Japanese commanders had committed suicide, and the island was secured. The longest, bloodiest battle of the war was over and so was the war. Japan capitulated within a month, and shortly thereafter Bart was shipped to the States and headed home.

Sitting there on the train, lost in his reverie and guilt, he had hardly noticed the young couple who had come into the car and taken the seat opposite him. He was jolted out of his mental anguish abruptly when the young fellow spoke. "Sir, I see by your ribbons that you've been on Okinawa," he said. "I'll bet that was exciting."

Bart slowly looked the young fellow over. He couldn't have been over 18, was dressed in a Navy uniform that had recently been issued. About the age of the young Navy men who had shot Smalley and Lewis down, Bart thought. Exciting? How stupid can you be! He was about to give the young sailor an angry retort.

Then he looked at the girl sitting with him. She was about the same age, blond hair and blue eyes, with the proud and adoring look of a bride when she looked at the young man beside her. He could see Ruth when they were first married, and imagine what it would be like to hold her in his arms again, to kiss her and smell the fragrance of her hair, to surround himself in the security of a love that would smother this depression which had engulfed him since Miller's death.

He had paused so long since the young sailor had addressed him that it was almost becoming awkward, when Bart quietly replied, "Exciting? I suppose some would call it that."

The Peril of Progress

HE HAD AWAKENED AT first dawn. During the night the oppressive heat had subsided and he had been able to get some sleep toward the morning. Rob, his bunk mate, was already dressed and about ready to go to chow. It was Rob's stirring that had awakened him, he guessed. They bunked just below the fantail where some of the anti aircraft guns were, and he could hear the crews already working at their stations. Rob was talking as he made his bunk, and when he had finished and was waiting for his roommate, he told Rob to go on to breakfast and he would catch him there.

Rob was his wingman, originally from a small town in Texas. They had been together since they were first commissioned a couple of years ago, and had that easy relationship that exists between men bonded by a trust which has been cemented by a shared hazardous occupation.

He went to the head and shaved, returned to his quarters and dressed, made his bunk and headed for the galley for breakfast. He wasn't in any hurry. They had been briefed the evening before, and he knew that Rob and he had drawn the last patrol of the day. The ship had been in Japanese waters for some time now, and they were sending out patrols from before dawn to after dusk. On his way to the galley he heard the thump of planes landing on the deck. It must have been the first patrol of the morning coming in. They had been catapulted off before dawn and had been out close to four hours. Both the Corsairs and the TBFs shared in the scouting. They fanned out in about a 120-degree radius in front of the carrier and were staggered in their timing, so the planes were being catapulted off and taken on periodically during the day.

Rob had just about finished his breakfast when he arrived. Several of the fellows were engaged in a conversation with Barker, one of the LFOs who had a phonograph in his cabin and some of the latest recordings. Barker was talking about his Frank Sinatra records, and some of the fellows had been to his room the night before listening to his collection. It was a popular place to hang out when Barker was off duty. The conversation gradually ran out as the breakfast finished, and the men drifted off to the ready room. Rob had already left. He talked a few minutes longer with Barker. Barker was off duty until noon when he relieved Duncan, the LSO who was presently on duty.

After he finished talking to Barker, he went out on the deck on his way to the ready room. The heat was already beginning to precede the rising sun, and the breeze from the wind coming over the flight deck was something to be savored while you could. You knew it would soon be gone when the sun rose enough to send scorching tropical heat bouncing off the deck into your face. But for now he thought, enjoy it while you can. There wasn't a ripple on the waters; it would have looked like a sea of glass if it hadn't been for the huge swells that kept rising and falling. A few porpoises, which had been traveling alongside the ship, broke the water every once in a while and caused flying fish to take to the air and glide for a bit before gravity destroyed the fuel for their fin-like wings. The steady muffled thump of the ship's engines turning the screw sent a steady vibration throughout the ship.

He walked past the bridge and went into the ready room. About a dozen or so pilots were there. Rob had his plot board out plotting his course for their patrol. Two Turkey pilots and some Corsair pilots from the last patrol were in giving their report. All was quiet. They hadn't seen a ship or plane. Their patrol was to launch at 16:30 as one of the last of the day, so he took the ship's relative position at take-off time and recovery time and worked his navigation problem on his plot board. Then he went over to Rob and they compared their work. They were in accord, so there was no necessity of them bothering with it further unless the ship changed its course.

He was just about to leave when Mike came in. Mike was the supply Sergeant, parachute man, all-around handy man. He had his arms full of goggles. "Look what we have a new issue of," he exclaimed. "Goggles with interchangeable lens!" He took a pair from Mike and examined them. They were quite an improvement over the goggles they were using. They were open all the way across which gave greater visibility; the lens were plastic and the goggles contained three interchangeable lens, clear, light green and dark green. The lens fitted in a slot which extended around the opening in the goggles and were secured by a snap when the lens were in place. They were met with general approval by all of the men.

Rob made the remark with tongue in cheek, "With progress like this we should win this war." He took a pair and closely examined them, then took out the clear lens and the light green lens and left the dark green. He ordinarily didn't even wear sunglasses when he wasn't flying, but those three to four hour patrols in the air with the sun bouncing off of the calm ocean were tiring to the eyes.

It was close to 09:00 when he left the ready room. He went to the flight deck and talked to some of the deck crew, then went to the flight surgeon's cabin to visit Doc Sukow. Sukow hated to fly, but as surgeon he had to be close to the landings on deck when the ship recovered planes. At that particular time Doc would stand in the door of the flight surgeon's room with just one foot on deck, ready to beat a hasty retreat into the steel walls of his cabin. He was an affable man in his late forties.

Drinking alcohol was forbidden aboard ship and Sukow was the custodian of the squadron's liquor supply, so he was a popular man. On one occasion the squadron had to fly into Saipan to get some parts for the aircraft that the ship didn't have. The only way Sukow could go along was to fly in a Turkey (TBF), so he mustered his courage and took a mussette bag full of the squadron's liquor along. When the pilot landed the TBF, he had gear trouble and one gear collapsed. The plane skidded sideways and the standing joke of the squadron was that before the plane stopped skidding, Doc Sukow was standing on the runway holding on to the mussette bag of liquor.

After talking to Sukow, he went below to the hangar where the mechanics were working on the planes. A pleasant little Italian by the name of Babe generally worked on his plane, and Babe was inspecting it today and fastening down some of the cowling as he walked up. They had a congenial relationship, and Babe asked him to take a look in the cockpit. He jumped on the wing and climbed into the cockpit. Babe was a devout Catholic, and he had put a medallion on a string and tied it to the setting knob of the clock on the instrument panel. He looked down and Babe was looking up at him with a big grin. He was obviously very proud of his accomplishment. He said, "What'd you think, sir? You like it? I put it where it won't get in your way."

A number of years earlier when he had been in high school, he had attended a baseball game between the local town team and an organization called the House of David. All of the members of the House of David had beards, which was unusual at that time. The local team beat them by a score of 12 to 2. He had noticed the left fielder of the House of David team, when they came in from the field for their turn at bat, always make sure he stepped on third base coming in. It became obvious that he did this out of superstition, thinking it would bring good luck. He kept doing this even as his team fell further and further behind. From that time on he eschewed anything that smacked of superstition or stood for good or bad luck. He even threw away an old rabbit's foot he once carried in his pocket.

He knew that Babe liked him and was sincerely acting in his behalf, thinking the medallion would be a lucky omen, but he just couldn't keep it there. He hesitated answering Babe, as he couldn't think of how to reply without offending him. After a long awkward silence, he replied as graciously as he could. "Babe, I really appreciate this, but I'm going to have to ask you to remove it. You see, I can't have anything that distracts from what I'm doing, and I'm afraid this will." He could tell Babe was disappointed, but he replied cheerfully, "Okay, sir," and that was it. He knew the medallion would be gone when he boarded the plane next time.

He left the hangar area and went topside and watched from the cat walk as the ship recovered another returning patrol, and then he went to noon chow and met Rob. After lunch they both went back to their bunks and rested for a couple of hours before getting ready for their patrol.

At 15:45 they were in the ready room checking to make sure there were no changes in their schedule. They rechecked their figures on their flight pattern and saw that it was still a no-wind condition. The heat by that time had become oppressive, and it would be a relief to get in the air where it could be somewhat cooler.

At 16:00 they brought their planes topside from below and rolled them up to and fastened them on the catapults. They were on a CVE, known as a Jeep carrier, and the deck was not of sufficient length for a loaded Corsair to take off from the deck, so all the planes had to be catapulted off. Rob was on the port catapult and he was on the starboard. The speed of the ship was another deterrent. In a no-wind condition as they were in at the time, all the ship's engines could muster was seven or eight knots at the most. The specifications for the Corsair required 31 knots of wind over the deck for take-off or landing. So the catapults were a necessity.

He climbed into the cockpit, fastened and tightened his seat belt and shoulder harness, started the engine and proceeded with his checkout. He carefully set his tabs for take-off, checked his controls, checked all his gauges, revved up the engine and checked his magnetos and prop. He gave the deck officer the thumbs-up signal and put the propeller in high pitch, put his right elbow in the pit of his stomach, got a firm grasp on the stick, put his head firmly back against the headrest, shoved the throttle full forward, put his left hand quickly to his chest to signify he was ready, then grabbed the throttle in his left hand and secured it at the same time by grabbing the throttle hook to keep his hand from being shoved back by the impact of the catapult.

Struggling against the force of the catapult, he was able to start flying about the time he reached the end of the deck. With only the seven-knot speed of the carrier furnishing wind over the deck, the plane dropped several feet before it built up sufficient air speed to pick up altitude. He lifted his wheels quickly after he left the deck to gain air speed. When his air speed picked up, he closed his flaps and quickly gained altitude. He banked to the left and Rob joined him. They climbed to 12,000 feet, and Rob separated from him and drifted about one-half mile to the left. The day was nearly cloudless and the ocean smooth, with only those swells which could hardly be discerned from their altitude. He set his propeller at a low RPM and his engine at a high manifold pressure and settled down to the monotonous task of staying alert and scanning the ocean for four hours.

The new green goggles helped considerably. They

were easier on the eyes, and the visibility was much better. One of the problems you had to watch out for was your imagination. If you didn't keep shifting your vision, you could easily imagine you were seeing things that just weren't there. After a couple of hours out, they turned on their base leg, and after completing that they started back. About an hour into their flight back, the sun had sunk so low in the horizon the dark green of the goggles was not needed, so he lifted them from his eyes to help his vision.

By the time they reached the ship, the sun was setting and dusk was settling in. As they entered the landing pattern, he broke off from Rob and prepared to land. When he opened his hood, the wind whipped his face and he pulled down his goggles and realized, with the dusk settling, combined with the dark green of his goggle lens, that he couldn't see the paddles of the LSO. He could see the ship okay though, so he thought he could make it. He had his height and his speed all right, but as he approached at a 45-degree angle where he generally picked up the paddles of the LSO, he just couldn't see the LSO, let alone his paddles, and he took his first wave-off.

He lifted his goggles and saw Rob land. He decided with his hood open and his goggles lifted he could keep his head pretty well in the cockpit behind the windshield and make it, and so started his second approach. He was doing just fine, but as he approached the carrier to pick up the LSO, he had to edge his head out in the wind a bit to pick up the LSO in the bend of the wing. When he did this, the wind whipped his eyes and filled them with tears. He had to take his second wave-off.

It was after the third wave-off he had to fight a bit of panic. He began to figure out the best place to ditch if he had to land in the water. He had seen a Corsair land in the water, and the memory of it wasn't pleasant. He had been running at full throttle and low pitch and didn't know how much fuel he had left. He had known pilots to run out of fuel on a landing approach and smack the bow of the ship, and it was messy. He even regretted telling Babe to take his medallion off the instrument panel.

He tried it goggles up again, and again the wind whipped his eyes into tears. When he took his fourth wave-off, he began to curse his stupidity. With full flaps, full throttle and in a rage, he whipped the Corsair around in almost a 360-degree turn to the landing. Through tear-filled eyes he blurrily saw the LSO give him a cut, and the tug of the hook catching the wire was the most beautiful feeling he could ever remember.

He was drenched with perspiration. He folded his wings and followed the deck man's instruction and taxied to the elevator. Duncan met him as he went into the ready room and asked him what had happened.

He explained the problem to him, and about that time the exec came up and asked him the same question. Before he could reply, Duncan cuts in and says, "Some guys have a hard time handling progress."

Johnny Green

AT THE LAST SQUADRON reunion I was talking to John Walker and asked him if he ever heard from Johnny Green. He told me that Johnny had stayed in the service at the end of the war and that he had passed away last year. Walker thought highly of him, as I did also. Walker told of a humorous incident which occurred after WW II at Cherry Point, North Carolina. Johnny and his family were living on the base when Marion Carl was the C.O.

When we were stationed at Cherry Point during World War II, Johnny had married a girl from New Bern. As I recall, she was a red-haired Italian. Walker said he didn't know if she was Italian or not, but she didn't deserve Johnny. Anyway, Walker said Marion Carl was a strict spit-and-polish skipper. Carl was an icon in the Corps. He was the first ace flying the old Buffalo at Midway, the first Corps helicopter pilot (he made the first flight without previous instruction), tested the first jets, and the list goes on. As C.O. of Cherry Point, he wanted everyone under his command to be as gung-ho as he was. This was hard for the average officer to maintain, so when Carl was driving around the base and saw some ragged edges he would take care of it personally.

This caused him to be known, in a whispered sort of way, as the sheriff of Cherry Point.

Johnny and his wife had several children by this time. They had base housing, and Johnny had flight duty away from the base at times. One of the times he was gone, General Carl was driving past some base housing and noticed that the lawn in front of Johnny's house needed mowing. He stopped his car, walked up to the house and knocked on the door. One of Johnny's kids came to the door and asked what the General wanted. Carl replied, "Your lawn needs mowing." The kid, about eight years old, asked him to wait a minute and he'd be right back. The kid ran back into the house and came back in a minute and told the General. "It's okay, you can cut the grass." Walker didn't know the rest of the story, but you can be sure the grass was cut.

Johnny was from Steele, Missouri. He was one of the original members of VMF513 and stayed with the squadron all during the war. He was about six feet tall, with dark hair and almost black eyes, a handsome fellow with a quiet manner. He wasn't bashful, but he was quiet and reserved, and he was always dependable and thoughtful.

He wasn't in my regular division. As I remember it, he was in Major Bales' division, but the Major didn't fly too much, and a number of times he would fly with some of the rest of us.

When we went aboard the carrier for our shakedown cruise, Groves, Green and I were the first three scheduled to be catapulted off the carrier. Groves was on the starboard catapult and Green on the port. I was right back of Groves to follow him on the starboard catapult. Groves' plane snaprolled immediately after leaving the catapult, and Groves hit the water. The ship went over him, and they then shot Johnny off and rolled me into the starboard catapult and shot me off. After seeing Groves go down, it gave me considerable comfort to see Johnny Green make it off the port catapult.

Another time the navy wanted to test a napalm mixture that could be used effectively on targets on the water. Green and I were given the assignment to demonstrate their effectiveness before some admirals and other brass aboard one of the battlewagons. There were two different mixtures for the napalm, one for land targets and the other for water. The armament boys were supposed to put the water mixture in our bombs, but instead they fouled up and put in the land mixture. Johnny and I had practiced a couple of hours on just how to make our approach to impress the admirals. We went screaming broadside of the battlewagon, dropped our bombs and pulled up in a wingover, expecting to see an impressive sheet of flame and fire. What we saw was more like someone had struck a match and the wind had blown it out. We returned to the carrier rather crestfallen.

Johnny and I were flying patrol off Saipan when we heard the war was over. We were given position sheets about every four hours to indicate the location of U.S. submarines in the area. I spotted a periscope come up, and no U.S. sub was on our position sheet at that location. It looked as if it were getting ready to surface, so I motioned for Johnny to circle while I went down to fire across its bow when it surfaced. I thought it was possibly a Jap sub that had heard the war was over and was coming up to surrender, and Johnny and I could claim its capture.

It all went according to plan. The sub surfaced, I sprayed the sea in front of it with slugs from six .50 caliber machine guns. Instead of Japanese coming out of the hatch, U.S. Navy men appeared desperately signaling in semaphore to let us know they were on our side. It was one of the war's thousands of goofs that the prop sheet hadn't gotten their position. We lost our opportunity to be heroes.

Johnny's children are grown and have gone their own way. I hope they are as responsible as he was, and I hope they recognized his true worth while he was with them.

Cousin Bob

IT WAS AT AN American Bar meeting in Dallas that I met this fellow. The lounge in the hotel was filled with lawyers from all over the country. When I went in the first evening, I elbowed my way through the crowd and found a vacant stool at the far end of the bar. The fellow sitting next to me had his back turned toward me and was giving his rapt attention to a heavy-set, fat-jowled lawyer, whom I took, from his accent, to be from some place in the deep South.

After listening for a while, I learned the fat-jowled lawyer was the prosecuting attorney of a rural Georgia county, and he was telling "war" stories of his experiences in that office. Every once in a while, after a particularly humorous anecdote, the fellow next to me would let out a whoop of laughter, slap the bar and order another round of drinks. The fat-jowled man would modestly accept his drink with delight as if it were small enough remuneration for the entertainment he was furnishing.

After one particularly vigorous whoop, my neighbor turned completely around and discovered I was sitting on his other side. "Howdy there," he drawled, "you been listenin' to ole George? Ain't he somethin'?" And extending his hand, "Ah'm Leroy Bissle from Molly Sprigs, Mississippi."

Molly Sprigs, Mississippi — that name took me back twenty years. I had just started practicing law, and my office was over the old bank building. The office faced west and caught the full force of the afternoon sun. We didn't have air conditioning then — just electric fans to circulate the air. During the summer that office would get oppressively hot. My secretary was fresh out of high school and looked much better than her typing. She chewed gum incessantly. I had been down to the drug store to get a cold drink and returned to the office about 3 p.m. It was sweltering, and I was trying to read some pleadings. After about fifteen minutes my secretary casually remarked from the next room, "You got a call."

I waited for additional information, and when none came, I replied, "So I got a call?"

"Yeah, it was a long distance call," she said.

By that time I had decided we needed to be in closer communication, so I walked into the reception room where she was busily filing her finger nails and inquired, "Did you by chance get the name of the person calling and where he was calling from?"

She stopped chewing her gum for a moment while she looked about her desk and said, "Yeah, I wrote it on the back of an envelope and it was right here, but it seems to be gone." Then she scooted back her chair and reached on the floor and triumphantly came up with an envelope and proclaimed, "It was from Molly Sprigs, Mississippi. He said to tell you it was from Cousin Bob, and it was urgent."

Cousin Bob! The last time I had seen Cousin Bob was several years before World War II. He was then tall, blond-headed, fairly nice looking, and his eyes were nearly always laughing. He had a ready smile, fell in love easily, quickly and passionately. His general approach to life was that it was either a lark or a beer bust. He rode its vicissitudes as smoothly as a frisbee in a gentle breeze. On occasion, however, he could be as impetuous as an unguided missile.

Sergeant Meyer of the Highway Patrol told me about the time during the war when Bob was driving the Trailways bus between Springfield and Memphis. He had been having a stormy marriage with his second wife, and was driving back from Memphis with a bus load of people. Just on the south side of Springfield, about the town of Seymour, he recognized a neighbor in a pickup truck who passed him going the opposite direction. He recognized the girl snuggled next to the neighbor as his wife of the moment, to whom he was hurrying home from Memphis to love and cherish.

Overwhelmed by the affront he was being subjected to, and recognizing rectification would require decisive action, Cousin Bob whirled his bus around in a U turn at the nearest driveway and gave chase to the pickup truck. The passengers, who had not been consulted or given a chance to express their views of this action, were at first perplexed, then concerned, and finally, after their lurching bus had forced two cars and a tractor-trailer rig off the highway, filled with stark, naked terror. Their affable driver had gone berserk. They were being piloted by a madman.

The driver of the pickup truck, mesmerized by the euphoria of clandestine love, was leisurely cruising down the highway, totally oblivious of the behemoth with the hot breath bearing down on him. Oblivious, that is, until the behemoth came alongside of him with horn blaring and brakes squalling, forcing the pickup off the highway and into the ditch where it came to a rest on its right side. The bus, with brakes locked, skidded to a stop shortly thereafter.

The dazed neighbor was slowly climbing out the window, which was now on top of the pickup, still innocently unaware of the cause of his sudden change of fortune. He was directing indignation and anger in a loud and colorful manner at the bus driver responsible. Then he saw the red-eyed driver bearing down on him with a tire tool in one hand and a rock in the other. The picture, which had been fuzzy a moment before, came into sharp focus. The neighbor catapulted from the pickup and began running toward Springfield with Cousin Bob in hot pursuit.

The neighbor had stepped on various parts of the errant wife's anatomy, including her face, while he was getting out of the pickup, so as she arose to crawl out the window, she was cursing the neighbor *and* the bus driver. She was halfway out when she saw her late companion running desperately up the highway to escape her enraged husband, and the awful reality of what had occurred became apparent. She promptly dropped back into the security and seclusion of the pickup cab.

The bewildered passengers had followed the driver out of the bus and now stood as silent spectators, watching the drama and trying to figure out the plot.

Cousin Bob was never one to carry physical exertion to the point of perspiration, so when he began to tire, he stopped pursuit and began retracing his steps to the main culprit who was ensconced in the cab of the overturned pickup. He reached the pickup in a dead heat with Sergeant Meyer of the State Highway Patrol.

The wife, cowering at the bottom of the pickup cab, hearing the stern voice of Sergeant Meyer, stole a peak outside, and when she saw her husband manacled and in the sergeant's custody, her courage welled. She came clammering out shouting dark threats and obscenities at her former beloved, so the errant wife was escorted to one patrol car while her ex-beloved went into another.

The Webster County authorities took an unsporting view of the occurrence and, in spite of Cousin Bob's cries of indignation, charged him with several felonies and misdemeanors. He made bond after a few days, refused to hire a lawyer, and eventually the charges against him were dismissed when no witnesses showed up for the prosecution.

That's the way he was. He seemed to walk in and out of trouble as through a revolving door.

So I made the call and heard an excited voice at the other end plead, "Man, get down here as fast as you can. I'm about to be arrested by the FBI. I'll meet you at the Peabody in Memphis in a couple of hours."

Now Memphis was 200 miles away, but the urgency in his voice was such that I assured him I would come as quickly as possible. So as soon as I hung up the telephone, I called my wife, told her to throw some things together, gassed up, picked up my bag and headed for Memphis.

Four hours later, I had just thrown my bag on the bed in my room at the Peabody when there was a sharp rap on the door. I opened the door and there stood Cousin Bob and a very nice looking blond woman in her middle twenties.

"Boy, am I glad to see you," Bob exclaimed as he threw his arms around me and engulfed me in a hug that reeked of stale cigarette smoke and beer. "I want you to meet my wife, Sue," he continued as I stepped back. "Honey, this is Cousin Dick I've talked about so much."

Cousin Bob had changed some since I had seen him last. His face was more florid and so were his eyes, but he had the same ready smile and easy manner. His wife, Sue, was a well-figured honey blond, a rather tall, nice-looking girl with a fair complexion, big blue eyes and a nice smile. She acknowledged the introduction with a syrupy Southern accent.

"Ah'm shure glad to meet yuh," she said, extending her hand. I detected her perfume was much more conducive to a hug than Bob's. I shook her hand and exchanged the usual pleasantries, then turned to Bob and queried, "What's this with you and the FBI?"

"That's a long story, Cousin," he countered. "Sue is going to drive our car back home while I ride with you. I'll tell you all about it on the way. Just give me that bag and let's go. I've already checked you out of the hotel." I left my key at the desk, and we escorted Sue to her car and watched her drive away. Then Bob and I started to Molly Sprigs. We rode in silence for several minutes. Finally Bob lit a cigarette, inhaled deeply and began his story.

"You know I drove a bus from Springfield to Memphis during the war. I got fired two or three times, but they kept hiring me back when their other drivers were drafted. That's where I met Sue. She got on the bus one day and sat behind me as I was driving. I began talking to her and found she had never been married. That was it. It was love at first sight. When you talk to her, you don't need to bring up my being married before, hear? She doesn't need to be bothered by that. Anyway, I was divorced at the time, and Sue was just right for me. She had a job with the Production Credit Association in Molly Sprigs and was making $125 a month. We decided to get married, and I left the bus company and moved to Molly Sprigs.

"There was a fellow in Molly Sprigs who owned a furniture store. His name is Marion Johns. He also had some jukebox and pinball routes. Marion is about 55 or so, and his wife died a year before Sue and I were married. Shortly after Sue and I were married, Marion married again. Marion's new wife was just 22 years old, and with their honeymoon and everything, Marion decided he needed some help. He hired me to run his jukebox and pinball routes. I changed the records and robbed the machines. He paid me $100 a month. With both of our salaries, Sue and I were doing pretty good. I was able to run the routes and still get plenty of fishing in. I learned to repair those machines, too. He used to have to take a broken machine to Memphis to have it fixed, but I got to where I could repair one as well as anyone.

"I thought by my saving him all that repair cost he could pay me a little more, so I hit him up for a raise. He agreed with me, and you know what raise he gave me?" Then convulsing with laughter, Bob said, "Two dollars a month! He paid me $102 a month.

"Now our county is a no-gambling county, so all of

the gambling on Marion's pinball machines had to be under the table. No one paid any attention though, and Marion is president of the Chamber of Commerce. He belongs to the Rotary Club, too. Why, even the sheriff would bet on those pinballs, and he's a wonderful man. Name's Bert Lucas and he has just been wonderful to me," Bob said with a heavy emphasis on the wonderful. "Just got through building himself a beautiful house. I'm going to be sure you meet him."

"Be glad to," I replied impatiently. "But what has this to do with you and the FBI?"

"I'm getting to that, Cousin," Bob resumed. "You see, the sheriff and I got to be good friends. He's really a likeable fellow. We got to fishing together quite a bit, and he'd come over to the house and drink beer. He's just a regular. Well, he was naturally interested in what I did and how much money those pinball machines would bring in to Marion every week. He's like that, just interested in people and their business. When I told him that Marion was just paying me $102 a month, he thought it was a shame. He knew Marion was well fixed and could afford to pay me what I was worth to him. Bert is fair that way. He doesn't want to hog anyone. I've seen him come out on the short end lots of times, just to be fair.

"I guess he got to thinking how stingy Marion had been, for one day when we were fishing he told me he had an idea how I could make a lot more money out of the routes I ran for Marion, and I didn't have to cheat him either. He said he knew a fellow in Memphis who would sell him some slot machines on credit, and he'd let me set those up in the same locations where Marion had his machines. I could take care of them, rob them for him and he'd pay me $50 per week. There he was paying me twice as much as Marion was right off the bat. Of course, we had to keep it quiet that the slots belonged to the sheriff, because some people wouldn't understand, it being a no-gambling county and against the law.

"So I picked up the machines for Bert in Memphis. I put them in the locations at night, so there wouldn't be too much talk. Nearly all the locations were glad to have them, but a few were afraid they might be raided. They were all right in a few days though. You see, Bert would drop in and act like they'd always been there. He'd casually start playing the slots, and first thing you knew everybody was at ease and didn't worry about being raided. That's Bert all over. He's sure a great guy.

"Bert paid just like he said he would, too. I'd have to keep his money separate from Marion's. After a few weeks Bert didn't go around the locations anymore. In fact, he didn't come to my home either, and he seemed to be too busy to go fishing anymore. I'd meet him at night once a week down by the bridge and give him the slot's take. Nearly everyone thought those slots were Marion's. Marion didn't even know the slots were there. His new wife was kind of babyish and insisted on him staying around the house. She'd hardly let him go down to the furniture store.

"Those slots were all nickel and dime, and I saw when I rolled the coins they were making good money. The locations liked the extra income they brought to them, too. Everything was going great, and with the extra income, I was making more than Sue, and we were able to make a down payment on a new house. Sue painted the bedroom a pretty red. You'll get to see it.

"Well, some of the locations asked me why we just had nickel and dime slots and no two-bit ones. I got to thinking that Bert and I were such good friends he probably wouldn't mind if I got some two-bit slots of my own and set them in beside his. He never went around the locations anyway, and I'd still do all the work. I even thought I might cut down on what I was charging him to service his slots.

"The more I thought about it, the more sense it made. Bert wasn't no hog. He didn't mind you making a little on a deal, too. In fact, he always said he didn't. I didn't want to worry him with it, so I just went to Memphis and bought three two-bit slots on my own, and set them up in some locations beside Bert's. The locations still thought they all belonged to Marion.

"You know, those things made so much money I was able to buy twenty more, and in just a short time I had one in every location. Everything was really going great. I was making more money than I had ever dreamed of. Bert's take had fallen off a bit, but he was still doing good and he didn't complain. Bert's really not a greedy type. I bought a Cadillac for Sue and one for me, and Sue quit her job at PCA. I was carrrying $3,000 to $4,000 around in my pocket so I wouldn't run out of cash. Marion and his new wife were happy, Bert was happy, and everything was going great guns.

"I think it was just after I bought my third Cadillac that Bert called me and said he wanted to see me, so I drove over to the jail in my new Cadillac so Bert could see it. He always liked to see a fellow do well, and I figured he'd be interested in it. But you know, Bert hardly looked at the Cadillac. He just crawled in beside me and said he'd like to ride by and look at some of the locations. He told me to go to Sam's Tavern first, and I don't think he said two words all the way there. When we got there, we went in, and Bert just looked around a bit without saying anything, and then walked out and got in the car and didn't say anything for a minute or two. Finally he said, 'How many those two-bit slots you got?'

"I told him and explained I knew he wouldn't mind as I was still taking care of his and was keeping the money separate. He said he was awful hurt I hadn't told him — that I was getting the long end of the deal. That he was having to pay half of his take to the prosecuting attorney, and it just hadn't been fair for me to get all my take, and him having to pay the prosecutor half of his. That in a way, he'd been carrying me because the prosecutor didn't even know some of the slots were mine.

"Well, I could see he was awful hurt, and I really felt bad about not telling him. But you see, I didn't know he was having to pay half of his take to the prosecuting attorney, and I explained this to him. He's such an honest guy. I didn't want to cheat him, and I told him so. I even told him to figure out what he thought my half to the prosecuting attorney would be, and I'd pay him back even if I had to sell one of my Cadillacs.

"He thought a bit, and it was then he suggested we just be partners in the whole thing. He said he'd figure up the cost of his slots, and I could figure up the cost of mine, and he'd figure up my half of what he'd paid the prosecutor, and then we'd settle up and be partners. He thought it might be better for us to get our figures together and meet some place in Memphis to go over them. He thought that since I was going to be the one who serviced the slots, it might be better if people in Molly Sprigs didn't see us together too much. Bert just doesn't like to stir up gossip.

"I thought it was a wonderful idea. You couldn't have a better partner than Bert. So we agreed to meet in a couple of days at a café in Memphis called Brady's. It had booths that were kind of private, and we met there at noon a couple of days later.

"You know we had just got our figures out and had started to go over them when who should come up but Marion Johns. He just slipped in beside the sheriff and sat down and said, 'Howdy, boys, hope this meeting ain't private, is it?'

"Bert quickly stuffed his figures in his pocket, and I did, too. I could tell Bert was upset, but he acted friendly to Marion and said surprised like, 'Why, Marion Johns, what you doin' in Memphis?'

"Marion replied, 'You boys have a heap of figures there. You doin' business together?' Then without waiting for a reply, he added, 'Me? I'm here in Memphis to see about getting some slot machines repaired. Bill Keeter got drunk in Charlie's place last night and tore a couple of 'em up.'

"Bert's face flushed and he sputtered, 'Marion Johns, you don't own no slots and you know you don't. Besides, they're illegal.'

"Marion said, 'Well, you know I didn't think I did either, but Charlie thinks I do, and so does everyone else in the county. Seems like they're scattered all along my jukebox routes. The only trouble is, someone besides me is robbing them. Another thing that's kind of bothersome is they seem to be taking some of the business my pinball machines used to get.'

"Then he looked at me and said, 'Wouldn't you say so, Bob?'

"Well, you know he had me there, for I had noticed when I robbed Marion's machines that his take had gone down some since we put the slots in. 'That might be, Marion,' I said.

" 'Yes, that might be,' Marion replied. 'And you know, boys, the only way I can figure out to bring my take up on those pinballs is to take my slots out.'

" 'Well, now hold on a bit there, Marion,' Bert said. 'You ain't going to pull that. You know blamed well them slots ain't yours. Ain't I always treated you fair? You been gamblin' them pinballs ten years now, and we've always split fair and square. And I always took care of the prosecuting attorney out of my share. Besides,' he added, 'when things is illegal, that makes it my business.'

" 'Bert, you didn't hear me clear,' Marion said. 'I ain't complaining about our arrangement. What I'm saying is, after I spent ten years of my life building up a little business with my pinballs, somebody has used my spots to slip in some slots, and all my locations think it's me, and they're taking my business. Now I think the only fair thing would be for whoever slipped those slots in my spots to, let's say, compensate me for the inconvenience they've caused me, not to mention the loss of trade, and having my name associated with out-and-out gamblin'.'

"You know, that was the first I knew Bert was partners with Marion on the pinballs. I knew all the spots kept chits, paid off the pinball winners in cash, and the losers had to pay the locations, but I didn't know Bert was a partner until right then. I began thinking maybe that was why Bert asked me so many questions about that pinball take of Marion's when we went fishing.

"Bert replied cautiously, 'What kind of compensation you talking about, Marion?'

" 'Well, I figure since the locations are mine, and the locations think the slots are mine, whoever owns those slots ought to give me about half of the take, to be fair,' Marion answered.

" 'You'll just have to forget that,' Bert sputtered. 'The owners of them slots ain't about to give you half. That's more than they're makin.'

" 'Did I hear you say owners, Bert? Plural? Do you mean to tell me that you let this pinhead have half of those slots?' Marion said, jerking his thumb toward me.

"That made me pretty sore, and I was about to say something to Marion, but Bert raised his hand for me to be quiet and answered, 'Yes, that pinhead and me are partners on the slots, and that pinhead has been keepin' you in business for the last three years. And that pinhead is the only one in Mississippi that can repair them pinballs and slots. Now if you want a deal, we'll give you a deal. It will be a three-way split and you throw in the jukes and pinballs. We pay the locations their cut and split the rest four ways. One part goes to the prosecuting attorney and the other three parts equal split between us.'

"That gives you an idea how fair and honest Bert is. Well, Marion took the deal, and that's how we all came to be partners. I kept running the routes and repairing and robbing the machines, and we were all doing pretty good. Instead of meeting Bert by the bridge once a week though, we'd drive separately to Memphis once a week and make the split there. Bert always took the prosecuting attorney's share, because for some reason or other he didn't want to meet with us.

"Well, yesterday about noon, Bert comes all excited and tells me that the prosecuting attorney had got word to him that the FBI was wanting to talk to Marion about some slot machines he owned. Seems like there was some federal law that required you to register a gambling device if you crossed a state line with it. You were supposed to tell where you were taking it, and stuff like that. 'Course we couldn't do that because our county is a no-gambling county. Bert said the prosecuting attorney told him they were going to start looking for slot locations the first thing in the morning. The FBI was keeping it quiet, and the only one they had told was the prosecuting attorney.

"That's why I called you. Marion wanted me to hire the same lawyers he has. He got one in Molly Sprigs and one in Oxford, but those guys wanted to charge me $1,000. Isn't that ridiculous?"

I began to have the uncomfortable feeling that Cousin Bob was looking for free legal service.

"I just made up my mind right then to call you, Cousin," he resumed.

"Now when we get down here about a mile further, we'll be getting to the bridge over the river. Slow down 'cause Marion and Bert are supposed to meet us there. The prosecuting attorney was supposed to get word to them this evening as to what we should do."

We drove that mile in silence. Cousin Bob was leaning forward, straining to see Marion and Bert beyond our headlights. I slowed when we reached the bridge. We crossed over and had driven a short distance further when some car lights flickered on and off twice, about 100 yards ahead.

"That's them," Bob whispered hoarsely. "Dim your lights twice, and then when you get even, pull over on the shoulder and stop. Then turn off your lights."

I did as instructed and in the darkness saw two shadowy figures scurrying toward us. Within a few seconds they had scrambled into the rear seat. Without waiting for introductions, one of the figures directing his attention to Bob said excitedly, "You got to gather those slots up tonight, hear? The prosecuting attorney says they's starting out fust thing in the mornin' to comb this county, hear? He says you committed a penitentiary offense when you brought them into this county, and you got to get them gathered before the Feds find 'em, hear?"

"Now wait a minute, Marion," Bob protested. "Ain't you forgetting that you own a third of those slots? How come of a sudden I've got to do all of this by myself. Man, it'd take one guy the rest of the night to gather those things. Most of the places would be closed by now, and you have to wake up the owners and all."

The other man spoke up. "Now, Marion," he said soothingly, "You ain't explained to Bob why it needs to be him that gathers them slots. It ain't like me and Marion are trying to load you up, Bob, it's just that we figure it's safer for you this way. You see, if all three of us gather the slots, all of the locations'll know that all three of us are connected, and you can bet your noggin some of them will spill it to the FBI. Then Marion and me won't be able to stand up for you. They think Marion owns them now, but they ain't seen him around, so they don't have no proof."

"Well, I guess that makes sense, Bert," Bob replied reluctantly, "but I don't think I'll have time. I'll have to wake them all up, and where am I going to put them?"

"I been thinking of that," Bert said. "You know if you'd give me a list of the places, I'd give them a call and give them a friendly tip that I heerd their place might be raided, and I was just trying to help them from getting into trouble. Then they'd be ready for you when you come around. We could get an extra pickup, and Marion and me could unload one while you took the other. I figure they'll be two loads or more. We can store 'em in Marion's warehouse in a corner of the loft."

"Hold on there, Bert," Marion stammered, "I don't want them slots on my place. They already think they're mine, and my place'd be the first place they'd look."

"Marion," said Bert in a patronizing manner, "there ain't no other place to put 'em. Besides, me and the prosecuting attorney'll know of any raid, and we'll be able to tip you off."

"Tip-off, hell!" Marion fumed. "How'll I move them things if I get a tip-off, and where'll I put 'em?"

"Now, Marion," Bert replied calmly, "we're wasting time. We can tote 'em up in the loft of your warehouse, and if we have to move 'em, we'll just move 'em, that's all. They ain't no place else to take 'em. You know I can't take 'em down and put 'em in the jail."

The logic of Bert's last statement seemed to overpower Marion's objections, and he grudgingly agreed to Bert's plan. Bob said if that was the plan, he'd better get going. The two men left the back seat of our car and melted into the night. Bob told me to take off as fast as I could for Molly Sprigs because time was short. I did and fifteen minutes later we entered the outskirts of town. Bob's house was situated on the west side of Molly Sprigs. When we reached the house, he jumped out of the car, grabbed my bag, told me to hurry, and bolted into the house. I was not far behind. Sue was waiting for us at the door.

"Haven't time to talk to you, honey. Something important has come up, and I have to meet Marion and Bert at Marion's. Take care of Cousin for me, and I'll see you later. I'm taking the pickup," Bob related quickly. He gave Sue a husbandly kiss and was gone.

Sue showed me to my room. I exchanged a few pleasantries with her, then excused myself and went to bed. I was soon enjoying the sleep of the uninvolved.

The sun was well up when I awoke the next morning. I dressed and went out into the kitchen where I found Sue at the kitchen table drinking coffee. She was barefoot and wearing bright red pajamas and housecoat to match. "Mornin', suh," she purred, favoring me with a lovely smile. "Hope you slept better than ah did. That Bob didn't show 'til 'bout daybreak. He's still sleepin'. You sit down here and ah'll fix you some breakfast."

With that she arose, brought me a cup of coffee and began preparing breakfast. I was about through with my coffee when Cousin Bob came in barefoot and groggy, still clad in his pajamas. His eyes were red and hair disheveled. He wearily sagged into a chair and asked Sue, "Honey, please rush me a cup of that coffee or I'll die right here before your very eyes. Man, what a night!"

"Marion's wife wouldn't let him leave the house after he went home. He was supposed to help Bert unload those slots and carry them to the loft, so I had to help Bert. Then Bert had to leave and go meet the prosecuting attorney about 3 a.m., so that just left me. On the second load I had to gather those things and then unload and carry them up to the loft of Marion's warehouse all by my lonesome. I never was so tired in my life. Honey, fix me a couple of those eggs, too, will you? What time is it? I'm supposed to meet Marion down at the furniture store at 11. Bert's going to get word to him from the prosecuting attorney as to what's going on."

"You still have plenty of time, sugah, it's just goin' on 10," Sue answered as she poured him a cup of coffee and then proceeded to fix his breakfast.

After breakfast we rode in one of Bob's Cadillacs to Marion's furniture store on the town square. We were met at the door by a worried looking little man in his middle 50s. He stood about five feet eight inches in height and had the pouch of middle age. The day was beginning to get warm, and he was perspiring. His face was florid, and every once in a while he'd take off the short-brimmed straw hat he was wearing and fan himself with it. On these occasions I saw he was bald with a little fringe of gray hair around his head. His eyes were small and pale blue. They were nervously darting from Bob to me, up and down the street and then back again. He wore a rumpled, blue-striped seersucker suit. He was a tobacco chewer, and the overflow had stained the corners of his mouth. He shot a nervous glance at me, nodded in the way of acknowledgment, and then directed his remarks to Bob.

"Where you been, boy? I just seen Bert and he says the prosecuting attorney sent him word they're going to raid my place tonight soon as I close up. You know what that means, boy? It'll be all over town." He took off his hat and began fanning. His voice almost broke as he said worriedly, "What'll the boys at Rotary think?" Tears welled up in his little blue eyes and he added, "Oh mah, I might even have to resign as president of the Chamber. You know what you have to do, boy? You got to move them slots out of that warehouse befo' night!"

I could see that this agitated Bob. His voice began to quiver a bit as he answered. "Oh, no, you ain't laying this on me, Marion Johns. I spent all night gathering those slots without hardly any help, and now I'm not going to load them up by myself. Besides, in broad daylight everybody will see anyway, and it won't do any good."

Marion saw Bob was becoming riled, so he mollified his approach and replied, "Now, Bob, don't get all het up. I couldn't hep you last night, though Lord knows I wanted to. I figure we can take my covered truck and back up to the warehouse like we're just loading furniture. We can put the slots in front and some furniture behind, and then you can drive over to Oxford like you're making a delivery. You can get a motel room over there and stay the night. Then we'll get word to you after the raid and you can bring 'em back tomorrow. Why, I'll even pay for the motel. If we don't move 'em, they're goin' to tie you and me both with 'em when they raid the warehouse. Here's $5 for the room," he said, sticking a $5 bill in Bob's pants pocket. Then he added, "You keep track of your meals, hear? I'll even pay you for them when you come back tomorrow. Be careful with that truck, hear? The key's right on the floor by the seat. Better stay at the Southern Motel, so we'll know how to get in touch, if need be. You drive down and back up to the loading door, and I'll be right down to hep."

Bob seemed convinced, and I walked with him over to the truck. I told him I'd rather not have any part of watching what was going on, so I'd drive his Cadillac back to the house and visit with Sue until he came back. He nodded in agreement, started the truck and headed around the back of the furniture store where the warehouse was.

I don't know how long I had been sleeping when a sharp knocking on my bedroom door awakened me. I finally found the bedroom light, turned it on, looked at my watch and saw it was 3 a.m. I called out in a hoarse voice, "Come in."

In came a bedraggled and defeated Cousin Bob. I had never seen him look so low. Gone were the boyish smile, the dancing eyes and the buoyant optimism that usually surrounded him like a cocoon. His face was flushed and his eyes were glistening as he fought back the tears. His six-feet-three-inch frame looked as if the rivets had been pulled loose, and he was sagging all over. He wearily walked over to my bed, slumped down on the side, buried his face in his hands, and began to cry like a baby.

As the sobs convulsed his body, I could imagine what had taken place. He had been caught red-handed, and now he was home to break the news to Sue. His present life was ruined, and an uncertain future lay before him. What a tragedy! It was an unsettling experience to see a big man sob as if his heart was breaking. I was engulfed by a wave of sympathy. I wanted Bob to know I really cared. I felt a lump in my throat and tears coming into my own eyes. At heart, he really wasn't a bad fellow, at least not that bad anyway. It would be sad to see him go to prison. I sat down on the bed beside him and put my arm around him to console him what little I could. As his sobs subsided, I tried to think of something soothing to say.

"Don't take it so hard, Bob. Time will pass more quickly than you think, and you're still young," I mumbled awkwardly.

"Oh, Cousin, it's terrible," Bob sobbed.

"I know, I know, it seems like the end of the world now, but life must go on, and this will pass behind you sooner than you think," I answered sagely.

"But those machines (sob) were so beautiful (sob)," Bob blubbered.

Machines? What was he doing lamenting the slots at a time like this? They had been his undoing! I began to get the feeling we might not be on the same wave length. I took my arm from around him. I stood up facing him and queried, "Machines? What are you talking about, Bob? Tell me what happened."

Bob took a deep breath, shook his head sadly and reiterated, "Cousin, it's terrible, terrible. Those beautiful machines are gone, gone! Do you understand? Those beautiful machines are gone."

I felt my tears and sympathy going, too, as I waited for him to explain. "You know I left you and Marion, and I loaded the slots in the front of the truck just like we talked about. I know nobody saw us. I backed that truck up flush to the loading door, and Marion and I loaded them. Then we put a bunch of furniture behind and some packing quilts, so you'd have to take all the furniture out to find the slots. Then I drove down to

Oxford just like we planned, and checked in at the Southern Motel."

"About 10:30 here came Marion and Bert, and they were in a lather. They said the FBI had searched the furniture store and the warehouse. They thought something had just been taken from the loft because the dust was all disturbed in one corner of it. They had asked Marion where his delivery truck was, and he had told them it was making a delivery. They had asked him where, and he said he swore he had plumb forgot. I guess this made them suspicious, so they had put out an all-state alert for the state patrol to find the truck. Bert said the prosecuting attorney had told him to get rid of the slots as quick as we could or we'd all be in one big pickle jar. Bert said he knew a back road out of town, so I followed him with my lights off until we came to a bridge over the river. Then we," he paused as if the memory was too much to overcome, "then we threw those beautiful machines in the river."

He sobbed, "I didn't even get a chance to rob them. I know they had at least $10,000 in them.

"After we got rid of the machines, they thought it best I just go back to the motel and come back home in the morning. So I left and I drove back to the motel. I had just got back to the motel and gone back to bed when here came the state patrol and the FBI. They got me up and showed me a search warrant and said they were going to search my truck, and what was I doing there and stuff like that. It made me kind of glad for a little bit that those machines were gone.

"They seemed awful disappointed they didn't find any machines. They asked me a number of times what I was doing there and where I was going to deliver the furniture. But I explained that I had just forgot where Marion told me to go, and I had decided to spend the night and try to find it in the morning. You know they never did act like they believed me, but after a couple of hours they left. I couldn't sleep any more, so I came home."

His sobs stopped as he talked. I could see the depression beginning to fade from his eyes, and as it did, the old buoyant nature started to return. Sue appeared at the door, walked over and put her arm around him. She bent over and tenderly kissed him on the forehead.

"Honey, would you please make me a cup of coffee before I die right here before your eyes?" he pleaded. Then added reflectively, "At least I came out a third owner of the jukes and pinballs. And come to think of it, I won't have to pay any damned attorney fees either!"———

"Molly Sprigs, Mississippi, Molly Sprigs, Mississippi!" I repeated as I shook the proffered hand of the man at the bar.

"You ever been to Molly Sprigs?" he asked with the same enthusiasm you'd expect from the secretary of the Chamber of Commerce.

"Yes, matter of fact I have. A number of years ago I met a fellow who ran a furniture store. Name was Marion Johns."

"Marion Johns? Did you know ol' Marion? Real good friend of mahn. Been dead a number of years now. He was a good ol' boy. Married a real young woman after his first wife died. Didn't live too many years after that. You know I'll tell you one on ol' Marion. I was prosecuting attorney of that county for a while, and we got word that ol' Marion was operating slot machines. You see we have a no-gambling county. Well, we heard that Marion had stored them in his warehouse when the FBI began inquiring. But, you know we looked all over for those machines and never did find 'em. He was slick, that Marion was. But he was a good ol' boy."

Dick at age 12

Dick and Lois riding on a horse

Dick and Lois riding horses, Dick on Paint

Dick and Lois after getting married in Corpus Christi, Texas

Dick as a young cadet (picture he sent to Lois)

Dick in Corsair getting ready to take off

(Left) Dick in California before going on aircraft carrier

(Below)
Dick on wing of Corsair he flew

*Squadron on aircraft carrier —
Dick is first right on second row.*

Dick flying Corsair in 1943
(picture given to granddaughter)

*Dick in front
of Corsair on
aircraft carrier*

One Eye

IT WAS BACK IN the spring of '48 when I first met Judge Tom Moore. I was studying law in the office of Green and Green, a two-partner firm of Will H. D. Green, who was then in his early 70s and known as Judge Green, and his brother, Dick Green, who was several years younger. Judge Green was well past his prime, but he had a wide acquaintance among the older judges in the area and was well respected. I rode with him on various occasions to keep the judge company and to observe court proceedings. He was a skilled trial lawyer and also had been a circuit judge for 12 years, so he had a lot to offer a young observer.

On one particular day, I rode with Judge Green from his office in West Plains, Missouri, to the small town of Gainesville. It was a beautiful spring day. The hills were speckled with dogwood trees in bloom and the buds of the oak trees were beginning to leaf out. I was driving and Judge began pointing out numerous houses along the way where former clients of his or of his father's had lived. It seemed as if at every other house there was a story to tell of some kind of litigation.

The Judge finally tired of reminiscing, so we drove

along in silence, simply enjoying the beauty of the Ozarks in the full thrust of spring. As we drove into Gainesville, Judge remarked, "Don't let me forget to have Judge Moore tell you the story of 'One Eye.' " Out of curiosity I inquired of Judge Green, and he told me it was the story of Tom Moore's father when he lived in Texas before and after the Civil War. By the time we reached Gainesville, I was eager to meet the old Judge.

Gainesville then was a small county seat town of 300 or 400 inhabitants. It had a town square, as was usual in most of the towns in that area. The courthouse was situated in the center of the square. Square and unpretentious, though not a large building, it dominated the town square. As with most rural courthouses, there was a fence around it with open gates at the entrance, and walks on the east and west sides. These ingeniously permitted a person to walk through, but kept any wandering cows off the courthouse lawn. It was a two-story red granite building with the circuit courtroom on the second floor. The tell-tale marks of having been built during the 1930s with W.P.A. labor were evident, and it was now beginning to show a general need of repair.

As Judge Green and I strolled up the walk to the courthouse door, he greeted all of the loungers sitting on the benches outside, and as we proceeded into the courthouse, he greeted all those loafing on the benches inside the courthouse also. They all seemed to be well acquainted with the Judge. At that time juries were often picked by the sheriff, and many of the loungers hung around the courthouse during sessions of court. Their hope was to be chosen for jury duty and thus get a little extra change. It paid dividends for an attorney to know and be friendly with those people, as you were very likely to see them on the jury of some case you were trying. So Judge paused to joke and palaver with all of them as he passed by.

When we first opened the door of the courthouse and went inside, I was immediately struck by the odor. All courthouses seem to have the same odor, a mixture of stale tobacco smoke, fresh and dried tobacco juice, floor sweeping compound, people, sweat, clothing and ink. But in this building — I guess because it was smaller than the usual courthouse and the people usually filled it up — the odor was particularly strong. We walked down the hall past the Magistrate's office to the stairway and climbed to the second floor to enter the circuit court room. Reaching the top of the stairs, we walked through double doors into the courtroom.

Court was in session, and there on the bench presiding was Judge Tom Moore. I quickly saw that he was a colorful personality. His gray hair was beginning to thin and looked as if a comb had just been carelessly passed through it. His face was round and rather cherubic, and his nose (somewhat larger than ordinary) was dominated by a little knob at the end, which seemed to be placed there for the express purpose of preventing his glasses from sliding off. His eyes were light blue, clear and penetrating. When he spoke, his voice was strong and resonant. It seemed that the court day was over and the large room was nearly empty. Judge Moore was sitting in his high-backed chair behind the bench, leaning forward and writing slowly and deliberately in the docket book. He looked up at us over his glasses as we came in; and as his face broke into a large grin, it was obvious that Judge Green was an old friend. He stood up and warmly extended his hand over the bench as we approached.

"Well, Will, welcome to Gainesville. How are you?" he asked as he vigorously shook Judge Green's hand.

"Very well, Judge," replied Judge Green, "and I'd like for you to meet a young friend of mine."

"Just a minute, Will, until I finish writing this order, and then we'll go to my chambers," he said. Resuming his slow and deliberate writing, he continued for three or four minutes. When he finished, he closed the large book with a thud and handed it to the clerk. Then he carefully climbed down the four steps that led from the bench platform to the floor, grabbed Judge Green by the hand again, and talking and laughing led us around the bench and out a side door to a rather sparsely furnished office which adjoined the courtroom. This was what he called his chambers.

Walking beside him, I judged him to be in his middle seventies. He was of medium height and stocky build. He closed the door and turned around. There were three chairs and a large table in the room, so Judge Tom sat down in the chair behind the table and motioned for Judge Green and me to take the other chairs. Judge Green introduced us. "Well," he remarked with a chuckle as we stood and shook hands, "it's about time some of you young fellows came along and took over. How old are you now, Will? You're younger than me by several years. I'm going on close to 80, and you know I still have two years of my term left."

After introductions we again sat down and he resumed, "Will, how's Dick and your oldest boy? What's his name? I never can remember that boy's name." As he looked at Judge Green with those pale blue eyes, he fumbled through his coat pockets as he waited for an answer.

"Yes, Judge, you have me beat a little," Judge Green replied. "Dick's just fine, though a little behind in his fishing; and Martin, my oldest boy, you know, is practicing law down South and making more money than his daddy." Then he added, "Judge, you're looking well. I was just telling Dick here as we rode over that you've had some wonderful experiences, that your father before you was the judge of this circuit before some of the counties were divided, and that you're well acquainted with all of the history of the area. I even told him that if you had time you might tell him that story of 'One Eye' you told me some time ago."

This obviously pleased the old Judge, for his eyes lit up and he rolled the cigar (which had been the object of his search inside his coat) around in his mouth in the slow and deliberate manner with which he had written in the docket book. He opened the drawer of his desk and secured a kitchen match from a box, proceeded to strike it on the bottom of his desk and lit his cigar. When he finished, he threw the match in the general direction of a multi-colored spittoon which was sitting on the floor about three or four feet from the desk; and it landed short of its mark among the rest of the debris around the spittoon, confirming the inaccuracy of the judge's aim of arm and mouth.

Then he looked at his watch and replied, "Why, yes, I reckon I have time. We've finished all the motions and we haven't much left. Let me tell the court reporter that we'll adjourn until 1 o'clock."

With that he rose from his chair and hustled off to the courtroom to speak to the court reporter. In a few seconds he was back, seated again in the chair behind the table. The story he unfolded soon removed us far, far away in time and place from the courthouse in the little town of Gainesville.

The old Judge placed his arms on the table and leaned forward. His eyes grew misty as his mind traveled into the distant past, seeing men and events and places of years gone by. He cleared his throat and then began in that strong, resonant voice.

"My father told this story to me many times when I was growing up. You know he didn't come to this country and marry and settle down until he was 35. He was in the war between the States; and after the war when he was in his twenties, he drifted over to Texas. Now it was a bit unusual for a Union man to be in that area at that particular time, but Father's folks were from the South and, you see, it was in the late sixties. He just didn't believe in breaking up the Union, so he fought on the side of the North. Then, when the war was over, he didn't think he'd be too welcome back in his home in Georgia, so he headed Texas way.

"Jobs were hard to come by and money was just as scarce, but finally Dad got a job with a fellow named Calhoun, who was raising cattle close to the Mexican border, not too far from the Gulf. There wasn't too much of a market for cattle at the time; but as the railroads began to expand after the war, markets began to develop and he worked for Calhoun for a number of years. Calhoun was a bachelor in his fifties when Dad started to work for him. He was a short, heavy-set man with coal black hair and blue eyes — a black Irishman, Dad said. He was a hard man, but he was fair. He wasn't given to many words, and he was tough as a desert mule.

"Calhoun's headquarters was not too many miles west of the Gulf and was close to the juncture of Beccero Creek and the Nueces River. A little Spanish village that later would become the town of Corpus Christi lay 100 or so miles to the east. The headquarters wasn't much. There were two adobe houses, an adobe bunkhouse for hands, an adobe cook shack and a blacksmith shop. Each adobe house had three rooms. Two of the rooms were each about eight feet square. The third room ran the length of the house and was about sixteen feet long and eight feet wide.

"The corrals, where the cattle were worked and the horses kept, were about 100 yards north and west of the bunkhouse. They were ingeniously placed between two little knolls, which hid them from the view of incoming stock until they were already trapped inside. The adobe farthest from the bunkhouse was where Calhoun batched. Sometimes he came to the cook shack to get something to eat, but most times he cooked his own beans and cornbread.

"The house closest to the bunkhouse was where Amos Keister and his wife, Rosita, lived with their two little boys. Amos was Calhoun's foreman. He was liked and respected by all the men who worked for Calhoun, and he had Calhoun's absolute trust. He was a tall, rangy man, about six feet two or three inches, was of a very muscular build, and weighed about 230 pounds or better. He was somewhere in his early thirties, had a ruddy complexion, and a shock of sandy hair that his wife kept trimmed rather close. His forehead was broad, and his hazel eyes were well set in a face that was a sculpture's model. He had large calloused hands and strong arms. Some said he had been a colonel with the Texas cavalry during the war; if so, he never mentioned it.

"In fact, he never mentioned anything much except what pertained to work or cattle or what he wanted you to do. Like his boss, he was fair, but he expected you to work when there was work to be done. If you had to ride for 20 hours to get it done, then you rode for 20 hours. He'd be riding with you though, always handling his share, and no one ever heard him complain. He had quite a reputation over the area and everyone called him Boss or Mr. Amos, everyone except Calhoun, that is. Calhoun called him Amos, but it somehow always sounded respectful.

"Talk around the bunkhouse was Amos didn't deal in foolishness, and you better not call his hand if you didn't have the hand to back you. Alfredo told about a little village across the border where Rosita's family lived. There were some banditos who rode into town periodically, shot up the town, robbed the people and raped their women. The village was practically held hostage by them. Alfredo said Amos and his wife took their first little baby down to see Rosita's folks in the village on an Easter day, and the banditos chose that day to ride into town and wreak havoc.

"He said Rosita's folks had four children younger than Rosita still living with them, two girls and two boys, and that both of the girls had been raped before by the banditos. So when the banditos started shooting, the kids crawled under the bed, Rosita's father and mother held each other real tight and began sobbing quietly. When Amos realized what was happening, he quietly buckled on his gun belt and crawled out a window at the back of the adobe. The parents' adobe was about in the middle of the village. There was just one street and the adobes were clustered together on both sides. Well, Amos got from the back of the adobe to the front just about the same time seven of the banditos came galloping up the street yelling and firing their guns. Amos was standing by the corner of the adobe and shot four of them off their horses before they realized what was happening. Then, he said, when one wheeled his horse and galloped back firing at Amos, Amos grabbed the bandit's leg as he rode by, jerked him off his horse and beat him to death in the road. The other two banditos kept on riding, and the town had been rid of their deprivations ever since. Amos never told this to Alfredo. Amos never told anyone. But Alfredo said he knew Rosita's father well, and Rosita's father who was there told him first hand.

"There was another incident, though, that my father saw himself not long after he started working for Calhoun. Bill Wells was an evil-tempered fellow with a mean reputation who lived about 40 miles up the Nueces and grazed a few cows. He picked up a hand who was as mean as he was, and they made quite a bully team. This hand went by the name of Short. Short wasn't a big fellow, but he was awful handy with a gun and quick to use one at the slightest provocation. Talk was that Bill Wells was a guerrilla during the war and Short traveled in the same crowd, and that's where they met.

"There was a rancher on Seco Creek by the name of Rube Weiber who had a little spot of pretty good grazing land that Wells tried to buy off of him too cheap. Weiber wouldn't sell at the price offered, but Wells told around that Weiber agreed on the price and then went back on his word. Weiber heard about it and confronted Wells one day when he met him in town. Short was with Wells at the time, and in a loud voice he declared that Weiber was a yellow liar, as he had been a witness to the agreement. Weiber never knew what he was up against. When Short yelled that he was a yellow liar, Weiber put his hand on his gun, and Short shot him dead before he knew what was happening.

"As it happened, Calhoun, Amos and Dad had driven a team into town to pick up some provisions. They were down at the livery barn feeding their horses when they heard the shot, and shortly after that the news of what happened. Now, Weiber had been a friend of Calhoun's, and when he heard the story, Calhoun made the statement to several standing around that Rube Weiber wouldn't lie ... that the shooting had been a put up job by Wells.

"News travels fast. It wasn't 15 minutes after Calhoun made the statement that the three of them — Calhoun, Amos and Dad — were walking down the road to Maude Handy's eating place when they saw Wells and Short cutting across from the other side to intercept them. They could smell trouble brewing.

"Calhoun said, 'Let's just slow down a bit so they don't have any trouble catching up.'

"They slowed their pace, and Dad saw people by the side of the road spreading the word that trouble was brewing. Wells and Short met them a few feet before they got to Maude Handy's, and it was Wells who spoke up.

"'Calhoun,' he said, 'I've just been told you called Short and me liars.'

"Now Dad was on the inside, Amos was in the

middle, and Calhoun was on the roadside. Dad and Calhoun didn't have a gun. Amos had brought his along as an afterthought. When Wells spoke, both he and Short were looking at Calhoun. Calhoun kept slowly walking ahead before he answered, and this kind of threw Wells and Short off a bit, for they had to back up to keep Dad and Amos and Calhoun from bumping into them.

"Then Calhoun replied in an even voice like he was just in an ordinary conversation, 'You heard right, Bill, that's what I said.'

"Then Dad said things happened so fast he didn't really see how they happened. All he knew was Amos had grabbed Short's right arm with one hand and with the other had stripped his gun from the holster and threw it to the ground. Then he raised his knee and broke Short's arm over his knee like it was a small board. He broke it with such force that the bone tore through his shirt. Then he calmly took the shells out of Short's gun, stomped on his left hand until it was a broken mess, pistol-whipped him with his own gun until he was unconscious, and then threw the gun across the road into the weeds.

"In the meantime, when Amos grabbed Short, Wells swung his head to look at Amos. When he did, Calhoun hit him with the force of a pile driver. He was driven back about six feet and fell unconscious on his back. Calhoun quickly walked over to where he fell, lifted him up by the belt about four feet, and saw he had no gun; so he dropped him and walked back and picked up his hat. He watched Amos finish making a mess out of Short, and then he said, 'Let's eat.' The three of them walked up to Maude Handy's and ate their lunch. Dad said he never heard either of them say a word about the incident to each other or to anyone else.

"Calhoun and Amos both were always helping someone who was down on their luck. A lot of times during December, January and February, there wasn't much to do. At a lot of places during the slack season the hands had to drift on to find grub at some other job, but Calhoun always fed his regular hands and sometimes those who weren't. Understand, when there wasn't work, you didn't draw your $10 per month wages; but the bunkhouse was there for you to live in until spring work started, and Calhoun would feed you.

"If anyone was sick or hurt, Amos always saw that they were taken care of. His wife, Rosita, was the same way. When a horse fell with Ramon Gonzolas and broke his leg, Amos rode all night to get the wagon at the ranch. He brought Ramon to his own house and put him in his and Rosita's bed. They slept on the floor until he recovered. Ramon always walked with a limp after that and wasn't much account as a cowhand, but Amos kept him on, patching tack and helping the cook. All the hands knew Amos would back them all the way if they just shot square with him and Calhoun.

"Amos' wife, Rosita, was a fine little Mexican woman. She must not have been over 15 or 16 when she married Amos, because she showed the youth of her early twenties, and her oldest son was about seven. She was a small woman, slender and short of stature, standing barely five feet tall. Her long black hair, which came almost to her waist, was usually clasped at the back with a silver brooch. Her features were sharp and delicate, and her voice had a soft, almost musical tone. She was quick in her movements, and you could see in a moment, being around her, that she adored her husband and two little boys. She kept her adobe clean as a whistle and had woven and plaited wool and goat hair rugs to cover its earthen floor and to decorate its walls.

"All of the hands liked Rosita. She was a kind, thoughtful person and was cheerful and friendly with all of the men without being too familiar. If anyone took sick with the fever or the flux, Rosita would bring them special broth that she fixed out of herbs until they recovered. Yet, with all her gentleness and lack of size, she had a tough, strong core. She rode a horse like an Indian, swung a lariat or cut a bull calf like a top hand.

"Once, when they were shorthanded, she rode with Amos, Dad and three other hands to work a little bunch over toward San Isabel Creek. They thought it would just be a short ride from the ranch and a short day's work, so they didn't take the grub wagon with them. Well, this bunch had drifted further west than they had anticipated, and they had to ride an extra day before they found them. By the morning of the day they were working the calves, they had run out of grub. They kept on working, and Rosita roped and dragged as many calves to the branding fire as any of the men.

"Along toward evening, she got pretty hungry, so when she dragged in one big bull calf, she jumped off her horse while Amos was branding it, castrated the calf and set its testicles on a rock by the branding fire to roast. She brought in the next calf, jumped down, ate one of the testicles and gave the other one to Amos. It didn't take long for the rest of them to follow her example, and they were able to finish working the cattle and to get back to the ranch after only one day without grub. The horses weren't that fortunate, but they made it all right.

"Harvey Finley was the cook and lived alone in the cook's shack. He was next to Amos in command. Harvey was a mulatto, and one of the most capable and intelligent people Dad said he had ever met. He was six feet in height and weighed close to 200 pounds. He was well knit with quick hands and feet. His repertoire of skills was endless. He could break a horse, shoe it, fix a broken wagon wheel or weave a basket. Also, he was the best trail cook who ever lit a fire. He was the only man Dad said he ever saw who could twirl two ropes at once while standing on the ground and catch something with each loop. Harvey's most valuable asset to Calhoun and Amos, though, was his judgment. He could figure just the right amount of provisions needed for man or horse under the most trying circumstance. He could judge what the weather would be and where the cows would drift or graze. He could judge the best location for setting up camp and the easiest and quickest way to get there. He could glance at a horse and tell you more about that horse than its owner could, and he knew how to handle men. It came natural to him. It was rather strange in a way, being that time and place, that all of the hands treated Harvey Finley with a respect bordering on deference. When Calhoun or Amos was absent, Harvey just easily and naturally took charge.

"Alfredo said Harvey's father had been a freeman, and he had grown up in the upper Brazos country. Harvey was like Amos and Calhoun, though; he never talked about himself. Harvey was treated as an equal by both Calhoun and Amos, and you could tell that all three men liked and respected one another. They worked easily together in a hard time and in a harsh place where life at the very best was extremely difficult and precarious. There was never any jockeying for position or rank. Everyone knew Calhoun was in charge, next was Amos, and then came Harvey. And any hand on the place would have ridden anywhere, anytime, at a word from any of the three.

"In addition to Amos and Harvey, Calhoun generally had 10 or 12 hands, and they stayed in the bunkhouse. During the slack season, sometimes two or three would drift off for a spell, only to show up a month or two later. Alfredo and Ramon were sort of permanent fixtures. They were there when Dad came and were there when Dad left. They were possibly in their early thirties and looked to be in their early fifties. They were tough and weather-beaten and cow-wise. Then there were young Tom Mask, who was about 18 or 19, Curly and Jim Stampman, Joe Diller, Tom Simpson, Charley Dray, Jose Ochoa and Dad, all top hands.

"As hands went, they were a rather quiet bunch. Oh, once in a while when some of them went into town, some would get liquored up, but this didn't happen much, and when it did, it was all over by the time they reached the ranch. Calhoun, Amos or Harvey sometimes took a drink on some special occasion, but that was it. They were mostly all business, and business meant work. Calhoun ran cattle on range that extended north and west from headquarters for almost 100 miles. This meant work, bone-weary work, riding from sunup to sundown. It meant coming in at sundown caked with sweat and dust, and after washing down your hard tack and beans with gulps of steaming black coffee, falling into exhausted sleep, sometimes without even removing your boots. Then, in the first gray light of the coming dawn, one's weariness appeased somewhat by a few hours of fitful sleep, sore, aching muscles would respond to the wake-up call, and each hand would arise and begin to work the stiffness out of his overtaxed body. Then after washing down similar hard tack and beans with similar gulps of steaming black coffee, one felt his strength resurge by the grace of the resilience of youth. By sun-up all were in their saddles riding to repeat with few variations the yesterday they had already endured. It was a life that quickly stripped away the superficial aspects of a man's character and left exposed only the hard core of what and who he really was. His strengths and weaknesses were quickly apparent for all to evaluate.

"About the first part of September, they'd gather up the herd and bring them to headquarter pens. Then they would cut out the calves, drive them to the railhead and turn the cows back on the range. This was the big drive of the year and everybody went out, that is, everybody except Calhoun. He generally stayed at headquarters and, of course, Rosita and her two boys were there, too. Before the big drive there were always a hundred and one things that had to be done. The corrals had to be repaired, horses shod, provisions secured for man and horse. Then these had to be packed right in the wagons. Every man had to check his riding gear to see that it was in good repair. Extra mounts had to be gathered, and each man had to prepare what few personal necessities he required for living, perhaps 30 days, in the saddle by day and on the ground at night.

"It was in preparation for the big drive that a new fellow rode into headquarters. It was about 4 o'clock in the afternoon and was still oppressively hot. The humidity was so heavy it felt as if one could cut it with a knife, and the thunderheads drifting in from the gulf were so thick they almost bumped into each other and towered higher than a buzzard could fly. They saw the stranger coming when he was a couple of miles away. He was taking care of his horse, walking him slow.

"When he reached Calhoun's adobe, he swung down from the saddle and led his horse to the watering trough. There, while his horse drank, he asked Ramon where the boss was, and Ramon told him Calhoun was down by the corrals. The stranger tied his horse and walked down there.

"Calhoun and Amos were together at the corrals when the stranger approached, and they both gave him a quick hard appraisal. He was not a large man, perhaps 5 feet 10 or 11 inches in height, of medium build, and walked with a quick easy stride. He was wearing short-topped boots — split out at the sides — and short spurs like the northern cavalry wore. His shirt and pants were of dingy, homespun cotton, and he was wearing a rather narrow-brimmed brown hat with a low crown. He was covered with dust from hat to boot, and he was carrying a short-barreled pistol in a shoulder holster under his left arm. It was the first time Amos or Calhoun had seen a man carry a gun in a shoulder holster.

"It was the man's face, though, that really grasped their attention. Black hair, flecked with gray, protruded under the brim of his hat and extended thick and tangled below his ears. He had several day's growth of beard; and, like his hair, it was black, flecked with gray and caked with sweat and dust. His face was long and angular. It almost seemed to come to a point at his chin. Where you could see his skin through the dust, it was the color of weather-beaten mahogany. He had a prominent nose which would have dominated his facial features if its dominance hadn't been supplanted by an old scar that extended from the hairline on the top of his forehead, down through the middle of his right eyebrow, through where his right eye had been, on past his cheek bone. It stopped about even with his mouth.

"Where the eye had been, the skin had shrunk back into the empty socket. It looked like the wound which had taken the eye had been sutured through the eyelid, for it looked as if the lid had been gathered there in the socket. His left eye was dark and piercing under a thick, black eyebrow, and the fatigue of many hours in the saddle, riding in the heat and dust, enveloped him. His lips were thin, and when he spoke, they saw he had lost one of his upper front teeth. He didn't fidget with his hands when he spoke. They hung easily and naturally by his side. His demeanor was one of self-assurance.

"He gave Amos a quick, piercing glance, and then, as if he immediately knew Calhoun was the boss, he fastened his sharp eye on Calhoun and without introduction said, 'Sam Morrison, up on Seco said you had a hand hurt and might use another rider.' Then he paused and added, 'I can work cattle, handle a horse and rope.'

"Amos couldn't place from his drawl just where he was from, but he judged he was from the north, maybe Missouri or Kansas. You didn't ask a man who he was or where he was from in those days if he didn't volunteer it himself. Calhoun judged he was from the Territory and paused a second or two as if thinking about it before he answered him. Calhoun was like that. He'd kind of pause before he answered a fellow a lot of times, as if he was thinking of what to answer. Actually, he was figuring the other fellow out, reading him you might say, and Calhoun could read a fellow pretty well.

"Calhoun answered him softly, 'Well, we did have a man break his leg a while back, but it's healed and he plans on going out on the drive, so I reckon we can't use any extra help just now.'

"Obvious disappointment etched the stranger's face. Then he spoke rather hesitantly, 'Wonder if you could put me up for the night and I could get some grub for me and my horse?' Then he added with the dignity of one too proud to take a handout, 'I can pay.'

"This time Calhoun responded immediately, 'There's an empty bunk in the bunkhouse and plenty of grub for you and your horse. Go to the cook shack and tell Harvey what you need, and he'll fix you up. No charge, my friend.' The stranger let the words sink in, and then said gratefully, 'I'm obliged.' Then he turned to make his way back to the cook shack.

"Calhoun and Amos watched the stranger make his way back toward Harvey. When he was out of earshot Amos queried, 'From Kansas, you reckon?' Calhoun hesitated in his way, watching the stranger for a minute before he replied, 'No, he's from the Territory. I've heard of some trigger workers in the Territory wearing a gun the way he does.'

" 'Ramon won't be much account in the saddle,' Amos remarked, then added as sort of a reluctant afterthought, 'I guess I could take Rosita, but we'd have to take the boys down to her folks tomorrow.'

"Calhoun kept watching the stranger walking toward the shack and mused half to himself, 'Chances are if he's a trigger worker, he ain't no account as a cattle worker.' Then he turned to Amos and said, 'Take him up the Nueces in the morning and drive in that little bunch that's close to the place. There ain't more than 150 grown stuff, and you can see if he's any account. Just you and him go.'

"Ramon showed him a bunk and gave him a blanket. The stranger nodded his approval, went and doused his head in the watering trough and rubbed some of the dirt from his face. When they sounded the chow call, he waited for everyone else to get to their place before he picked a spot and sat down. He ate in silence, and he left in silence. He didn't speak one word to anybody. He acknowledged when someone passed him some grub with a nod of his head. Nobody said anything to him either. They did all measure him out of the corner of their eye and wondered where he came from and what he was doing there. He wore that gun in the shoulder even when he ate, and that night before he lay down, he took his gun out, took the shells out and carefully wiped the dust off it the best he could and spun the barrel. Then he reloaded it slow and careful. (Dad said he saw it was a short-barreled .44.) When he lay down to sleep, he laid it in its holster on top of his shirt on the floor by the head of his bed.

"The hands started stirring the next morning when it first started to get gray light. There were the stretching, yawning, coughing, and all the wake-up noises that have always been heard in varying degrees when people first start a new day. The stranger's bunk, however, was empty. The only evidence that he had been there was the blanket neatly rolled, army style, at the foot of the bunk. When the breakfast call sounded, he appeared. As on the evening before, he waited until everyone else had taken their place before he sat down and started to eat. Again he ate in silence and acknowledged the passed grub with a nod of his head. He didn't say a word until Amos came in shortly after they started to eat. Amos strode up to the end of the table where the stranger was eating and said, 'Mister, when you're finished eating, we'll be ready to go.'

"The stranger nodded assent. Then Amos added casual like, 'By the way, Mister, what name do you go by?'

"Well, everyone at the table paused in their eating and strained their ears. The stranger, without looking up or pausing in his eating, answered softly, 'Folks call me One Eye.'

"Amos looked down at the fellow for a couple of seconds, then said, 'All right, One Eye, I'll meet you at the corral.' And those were the only words the stranger spoke during his second meal in the bunkhouse.

"That evening about 4 o'clock Amos and One Eye drove a small bunch of about 150 cows with their calves into the east corral. They brought them slowly as it was still pretty hot and muggy. Both of their horses were soaked with sweat, but One Eye's dun was breathing easier than Amos' horse. The dun was big and raw-boned and in good riding shape, not poor, but not fat either.

"They left their horses down by the corral, and while One Eye was unsaddling his, Amos walked up to the blacksmith shop where Harvey was shoeing some horses. Calhoun and several of the other men were there. As Amos approached, Calhoun looked at him quizzically and Amos answered his look. 'He'll do,' said Amos.

"Calhoun seemed somewhat disappointed in Amos' approval, and mused as if half to himself, 'Don't want no troublemaker.' Amos answered him, 'Won't be no trouble.'

"That was how One Eye happened to ride on the big drive. Dad didn't know when they told him, but he appeared more relaxed that night at chow. Still, he didn't talk.

"The next day was all hustle and bustle, because preparation was being made for riding out the following morning. Ramon had One Eye help him pack the wagons, and Harvey had him bring up some horses from the corral for shoeing. He responded to his tasks willingly and in a capable manner. He volunteered to help Harvey shoe some, and Harvey let him shoe one to see what kind of a job he did. After that, Harvey put him to shoeing several more. He did a good job, but he still seldom talked, never smiled, and seemed married to that short-barreled .44. He even wore it when he was shoeing horses. It was as if he thought someone would steal it if he hung it up, or maybe he had worn it so long he felt sort of naked without it.

"The men started out the next morning while it was still dark. They wanted to travel as much as possible during the coolest part of the day. Calhoun and Rosita and her boys saw them off. Ramon was driving the supply wagon, and Harvey was driving the chuck wagon. Both of the wagons had four horses tied to lead ropes behind, and Joe Dillar and Jim Stampman each led four extra. The plan was to travel west toward the Rio Grande, pushing the cattle from the north flank of the trip south, and then, when they got to the west end of the range, to start gathering them from the west and south and drive them back east to the ranch. The weather was beginning to cool some, but they still had to take it fairly easy on the horses. It was a trip that could take 30 days on the outside.

"The men worked in pairs at the start. They fanned out from the wagons to the north as they traveled west, and One Eye started working with Alfredo. His dun was a good horse and cow-wise, and One Eye took extra good care of him. He'd rub him down at night and scrape all the dirt from the leather on his hobbles so they'd be easier on his legs. He'd do little extra things like examine his hoofs two or three times a day to make sure no gravel was getting between the shoe and the frog. One Eye did his work well, but he never joined in any talk or banter. He answered when he was spoken to and that was about all. He did seem to go out of his way to help where he could. If Alfredo and he had worked their area out before the others, he'd always ride over where others were riding to help if he could, and he'd relieve Harvey of shoeing chores most of the time.

"After two or three days, the curiosity of the men gave way to acceptance; besides, the demands of the long hard days in the saddle stripped away the luxury of idle speculation. In about two or three days he was just one of the hands. There was one difference though; he stayed married to that short-barreled .44. He wore that gun in its shoulder holster no matter what he did, and there on the drive, he'd even sleep wearing the thing. Every night he'd check it and clean it the best he could. No one else wore a gun. All the other hands left theirs in the supply wagon Ramon drove. But after a day or two, nobody paid much mind.

"It was on the fourth day out, a couple of hours before dark, a kid rode into camp from the south. He was riding a little paint horse, so poor it looked like it could hardly walk. It was unshod, tender, and stumbled every step. The kid looked like he'd missed a few meals too. He was thin and pinch-faced with black eyes that had lost the sparkle of youth and looked at you with dull resignation, passively accepting what fate would toss his way. His thick black hair cascaded down his head under a torn sombrero. He wore the faded white homespun shirt and pants of a Mexican farmer. These were ragged and frayed, and his feet were bare in the stirrup. He had one of those Mexican saddles made out of wood, and he had it padded with so many blankets that it rode high on his horse. The kid could have been 13 or 18, it was hard to tell. He wasn't over 5'2" and he was all skin and bones.

"He walked his horse to the chuck wagon where Harvey was working. He took off his sombrero in deference to Harvey, and then he said softly, 'Senor, I could work for something to eat for my Panpaya, yes?'

"Then, when Harvey was looking him over, before he replied, the kid added, 'I work veeery good, I am veeery strong.' With that assertion, he drew himself up in the saddle to appear as big as he could.

"Amos was over by Ramon's supply wagon a short piece away when he saw the kid come up and watched him talk to Harvey. Then Harvey turned and motioned for Amos to come there. When Amos came, Harvey took him aside and said, 'The kid looks like he's about starved, but he wants to work for some feed for his horse.'

"Amos looked at the kid again, thought a minute,

and then said, 'If you could use him to chore for you on the drive, maybe we could feed him and his horse enough for them to get wherever they're headed by the time we get back home. You do what you think.'

"Harvey said, 'I can use him.' With that, Amos turned to the kid like he was addressing a man and said, 'Mister, you can help Harvey. He'll be your boss. You'll do what he says and answer to him. You'll get food for you and your horse as long as you work. We're going toward the Rio Grande and then back home, which is east of here. That may take three weeks or so. If you want, you can work until then. You can take your horse over to Ramon and he'll take care of him.' Well, the kid's expression didn't change, but his eyes filled and overflowed and two large tears slowly trickled down the dust of his face.

"He said softly, 'Gracias, Senor.' He rode his poor little horse over to the supply wagon and turned him over to Ramon.

"The kid's appearing did not escape One Eye. He had been tending some horses, and when the kid rode over to Ramon, One Eye sauntered over as Ramon was unsaddling the paint. Ramon was talking to the boy in a bantering tone as if he was a nephew or someone close to him. 'Ah, si, you always ride until your belly rubs your backbone? You feed your horse so many blankets on the back to fatten him, si?'

"The kid's eyes had brightened up, and he replied, 'Some nights in the mountains it gets veeery cold. Many blankets are good.'

"He saw One Eye looking over his horse, and he put one arm under his neck and started stroking the horse's neck with the other hand. Addressing One Eye, he said, 'Senor, Panpaya, he is a veeery good horse, si?' One Eye never looked at the kid. He just replied simply, 'Panpaya needs shoes.'

"Then he told Ramon that when the horse had finished eating, he'd take him and shoe him. Ramon, of course, didn't care, so after the paint ate a little grain, One Eye got the tools and shod him. Well, after that, One Eye couldn't have been any greater in the kid's eyes if he had dropped as a winged angel straight from heaven.

"It was amazing what a few good meals did for the kid and the horse, too, for that matter. In a couple of days, the kid was doing all sorts of chores around the camp. He'd fetch wood and water, get the wagon teams in the morning, hitch them up and unhitch them at night. He'd wait on Ramon and Harvey and everyone else who would let him. He almost hovered over One Eye, and One Eye seemed to mellow a bit after the kid came. He even talked to the kid some. One evening, though, the kid's curiosity got the better of him while they were eating their grub. The kid was right next to One Eye and asked innocently, 'How deed you get your scar, senor? You in one beeg fight?'

"About everyone stopped chewing their beans and stretched their ears to hear One Eye's reply. An awkward silence settled over the entire camp. All you could hear was the crackle of the fire and in the distance the snorting of a horse where it was tethered. When One Eye didn't answer right off, the boy saw that he had asked a question that maybe he shouldn't have asked, and he began to fidget uncomfortably. Then, One Eye said slowly, 'Well, a number of years ago, when I was a young feller, I had a real long sharp tongue. One day that tongue got out of my mouth, turned on me and slashed my face, and I had to bite it off or I guess it'd kilt me.' The kid dropped his eyes and didn't say a word. Nobody laughed; they just all went on like they hadn't heard. It didn't seem to make One Eye mad though. He still acted like he enjoyed the kid being around, and kind of being the kid's favorite.

"It wasn't but a day or two after that when One Eye took sick. He came down with chills and fever. He rode out in the morning looking peaked, and that night when he got off his horse he fell in a faint. They laid him on a blanket, and the kid brought him some bean soup and water. He couldn't eat, but he did drink some water. The next morning they had to move on, so the kid helped make a bed in the supply wagon, and they carried One Eye to the wagon and laid him in there. Before they moved out, the kid went out and dug up some kind of roots and brought them to Harvey who made a broth of tea out of them. The kid fed some of this to One Eye. From then on, taking care of One Eye was the kid's main interest. Oh, he did some other chores, but he'd never get far from One Eye for very long. He'd make that herb tea for him and feed it to him a spoonful at a time. He slept right beside that wagon and was up looking after One Eye several times a night. He took off One Eye's boots and pants and put all of his own blankets around him to make him as comfortable as possible. That kid looked after One Eye like he was a newborn baby. Somehow he found a rag and can, and he put water in the can and kept bathing One Eye's head when his fever got high. Amos saw that the kid was sleeping on the ground and had Ramon get him a couple of blankets, and the kid even put one of these around One Eye. One Eye never let him take his gun and shoulder holster off of him though, even when he was nearly out of his head with fever.

"This went on for several days, and some thought surely he'd die. But that kid's care and herb tea and One Eye's toughness finally began to tip the scales. One Eye's fever broke a couple of days before they reached the Rio Grande. The day they reached the Rio Grande, he was able to weakly crawl out of the wagon with a lot of help from the kid and Ramon, and he stayed up for a couple of hours.

"So far, the drive had gone pretty well, and the cattle they had pushed down from the north had already started to drift back towards headquarters. One of the wheels of the chuck wagon needed working on, so Amos decided to camp for a day and wait until Harvey could fix the chuck wagon before heading back.

"That night there was a more relaxed atmosphere around camp. The men were getting a few hours needed rest, and there was more bantering and talking than usual. That night One Eye was able to get out of the wagon with Ramon and the kid's help and eat a bite of chow.

"There was a moon, but millions of stars made a halo around the earth. In the distance across the Rio Grande, the candle lights of a little Mexican village twinkled in the darkness. The weather was beginning to cool some, so the humidity was not so oppressive. Everybody seemed to be in a salubrious mood.

"Well, the next day Ramon and Harvey worked about all day on the wagon, and toward evening they had it fixed. Amos said the next morning they'd start out bright and early.

One Eye

"It was Alfredo who suggested riding over to the Mexican village that evening. He said he thought he knew a fellow who lived there, and he hadn't seen him for a spell. He asked several of the men to go with him for company. Well, about everyone had been lounging around all day, so he had some ready takers. There were Dad and the Stampman brothers, Joe Dillar, Tom Simpson and Charley Dray who agreed to go with him. Before long they persuaded Amos to go, too. Before they left, Amos went to the wagon and got his gun belt, and then the rest of the men did, too.

"They started out before sunset. The village was about 30 minutes ride from the camp, so they reached it at dusky dark. The village consisted of not more than two dozen adobe houses and one street. Some children were playing in the dusty street as they rode up, and a woman carrying a jug of water quickly entered an adobe, glancing back nervously at the strangers approaching. Alfredo inquired of the children about his friend, and one little boy pointed out his house, and they rode up the street and stopped at the house the boy pointed out.

"Alfredo dismounted and called out, 'Ricardo Alverez.' The door opened in the little adobe, and a small Mexican man came into the doorway looking somewhat perplexed and apprehensive. When he recognized Alfredo, however, his face broke into a broad grin, and he embraced Alfredo. They began conversing in rapid Spanish, and then Alfredo turned to the group and announced, 'Ricardo,' he says, 'Tell your friends to tie up your horses and come into Ricardo's house.'

"So they dismounted and crowded into the little adobe. It was a small two-room adobe. One room was used for cooking and living area and the other for sleeping. Ricardo had a wife and three children, and as the men came in, the children were curiously peeking from the entrance of the sleeping room. A small table and two split-bottom chairs constituted the furniture in the room. A blanket served as a door between the living and sleeping areas. The floor was packed dirt with no rugs, but it had been swept clean; an earthen oven was against the wall at the right end of the room as you went in.

"The room seemed very crowded when all the men got in. They lined up rather awkwardly along the wall while Ricardo produced a bottle of tequila and passed it around. Ricardo's wife left the house, was gone for a little bit and then came back with another bottle of tequila. By the time that bottle went around, the men were relaxed and were either sitting or squatting on the floor against the wall, and conversation began picking up. Then the village people began drifting in, and the little room that was crowded to start with became jam-packed. A couple of men with a guitar, a mandolin and another bottle of tequila came in. After introductions and passing around their bottle of tequila, they started playing and singing. Then came some women with a big pot of beans and flat cornbread, then more women and men and more tequila.

"Before long, everyone was eating beans and cornbread and drinking tequila, and it seemed like more people kept packing into that little room. They lifted one young girl who was about 15 or 16 up on the table, and she did a kind of stomp dance on that little table while they all sang and clapped their hands. I guess the entire village joined in to welcome Ricardo's friends from the big Americano ranch.

"Well, about 11:30 or so Amos decided that they'd better get back before things got clear out of hand, so after several more toasts to their Mexican friends, the crew took their reluctant leave and rode back to camp full of beans, cornbread and tequila. Before they left, Amos pressed two silver dollars into Ricardo's hand.

"As they approached camp, talking and joking and discussing the evening, Alfredo suddenly let out a 'whoop' and fired his pistol a couple of times in the air, spurred his horse into a gallop and rode 'whooping' toward the campfire. Well, all the rest joined in, and they rode into camp whooping and shooting. Even Amos joined in. He was bringing up the rear. He 'whooped' and fired a couple of times in the air, and as he rode toward the campfire, he fired his pistol a couple of times into the ground.

"Ramon and the kid were sitting by the campfire. They had been waiting for the men's return, and when the whooping and firing started, they both stood up and were standing there grinning when the men rode up. When Amos rode in and fired into the ground, his second shot ricocheted off a rock and struck the kid square in the stomach as he stood there all smiles beside Ramon.

"The kid let out a cry and grabbed his stomach as he buckled over and crumpled to the ground. Ramon saw at once what had happened. He yelled for help and laid the kid out on his back. Amos was quick to see, too, and jumped down from his horse and ran to help Ramon. The rest of the men milling around gradually realized that someone was hurt and stopped whooping and shooting.

"A hushed silence came over the camp. The air of exultant celebration that had filled their spirit all evening evaporated, and men started gathering around wanting to help. Yet they were helpless to aid the kid. Amos cut through his shirt and pants, hoping against hope that the wound was superficial, but he discovered quickly that the slug had evidently flattened on the rock, had torn a gaping hole in the kid's stomach and had gone deep inside. The kid's eyes were filled with fear and his face contorted with pain. Ramon and Amos kept speaking softly and with reassurance to the kid. They got a bunch of blankets and put under him and covered him to keep him from getting so cold. There was not much else they could do for him, except get him some water to drink. He cried a great deal from the hurt, and in about three hours he died, grimacing from pain.

"One Eye crawled weakly from the wagon, walked to where the kid lay, kneeled down and stroked his face. The black eye filled with tears, and he blinked several times. Then, without a word he turned, walked back to the wagon and crawled in.

"Amos, Ramon, Harvey, Dad and several of the others dug the grave. They buried him deep and pilled a little mound of stones on top. It was breaking daylight when they finished, so they broke camp and started the drive back. That first day was a long one. They had been up all night, and when they wearily came into camp at the end of the first day, there was hardly a word said. They just ate their grub, wrapped up in their blankets and fell asleep. One Eye came from the wagon and ate with the rest in silence.

"One Eye started riding the next day. He was still

very weak, but he saddled his own horse and somehow managed to stay in the saddle. After three or four days, he was almost back to normal and was riding about as much as anyone else. It was after he got his strength back that he began staring at Amos when he came in at night. A pall seemed to have settled on the group. At first they tried not to pay any attention to One Eye's staring; but as the days passed it seemed to grow in intensity until everyone had a feeling of impending trouble. It even made a person uneasy when they got between Amos and that stare. One Eye did his work as he had done before, but now nobody really wanted to pair with him. When a fellow had to pair with him, he'd get away as soon as he could and drift over to help someone else. Several of the men got their guns out of the wagon and started wearing them while they worked. Amos never let on if One Eye's staring bothered him, and he never slacked off of telling One Eye where to work either. There was just one thing that Amos did differently. He didn't call him One Eye anymore; he called him Mister. He'd say, 'Mister, you start riding with Curley today,' or 'Mister, you ride far out to the south, there's always a bunch fed near such and such a place,' and One Eye would stare, but never speak. Amos had put his gun in the wagon and never wore it after the kid died.

"All the men knew that Amos felt a deep remorse over the accident that had killed the kid. They wanted to talk to him, to cheer him up and to tell him it was an accident that could have happened to any one of them, but they were men not used to expressing their feelings with words or communicating openly with one another. So they expressed themselves in the only way they knew how. They worked. Whatever Amos directed, they busted themselves to get it done and done well.

"It should have been apparent to anyone that all the rest of the men were with Amos 100 percent, but this didn't seem to affect One Eye. Every night his staring seemed to become more intense, and the tension in the camp at night grew so tight they were glad to see morning come. The tension released somewhat in the hard work of the day. Harvey got his rifle from the supply wagon and put it in the chuck wagon. Ramon and Alfredo started wearing their guns, and before long everyone in camp was wearing his gun when he worked, everyone, that is, except Amos. He continued to leave his gun in the supply wagon, and he continued to ignore One Eye's malevolent stare. While the rest of the camp walked around like they were stepping on eggs and speaking in hushed voices, Amos conducted himself with almost studied nonchalance, and when he spoke, it was always in a casual and normal tone.

"As far as the work was concerned, it went well. The cattle that had been pushed down from the north on the drive out had started drifting back to the ranch as they grazed south, so the riders didn't have to double back much at all. But there was no joy or exhilaration or light-heartedness in the work. There was such an oppressive tension in the air, such a feeling of impending trouble, that the work seemed doubly hard and depressing.

"That was the way it went until they reached Sandstone Spring. Sandstone Spring was about a day's drive from headquarters. Already some of the lead cattle would be coming into the pasture just west of the corrals, and Calhoun and Rosita would be looking for the main herd the next day. They were right on schedule.

One Eye

They always camped at Sandstone Spring going out and coming back. A clear strong spring of water came from the bottom of a sandstone outcropping, and the cattle, horses and men would get their fill of the cool, sweet water that gushed out. The spring itself was down in a little draw, and as usual Harvey made camp on the high ground just west of the spring. He drove in fairly early in the evening, well before sunset, and had supper ready somewhat earlier than usual. The men rode in and seemed to be in a better mood. I guess everyone was looking toward the end of the drive. They knew that headquarters was just a day's ride away. Then they would be rid of One Eye and that dreadful stare, and everything would get back to normal.

"But when One Eye came in, he resumed that same unwavering malevolent stare. Even this, though, didn't completely suppress the air of expectancy that enveloped the men, and there was some light-hearted banter among them for the first time since they started back. Even Amos joined in some. It all stopped though and a deadly hush came over the camp when they finished eating, for Amos casually strolled over to the supply wagon and came back wearing his gun.

"For the first time since they'd started back, One Eye stopped staring at Amos. Instead, he turned and looked toward the spring, and after a minute or so he stood up, where he had been sitting and eating, and walked slowly down toward the spring. When he reached the spring, he crossed it and went to the sandstone outcropping, leaned against the rock, rolled a cigarette, lit it and started smoking it.

"The eyes of all the men in camp were riveted on his every movement. Harvey edged over to the chuck wagon and lifted out his rifle. One Eye just leaned against the rock and smoked his cigarette. He didn't look toward the camp. He finished his cigarette, and when he did, Amos walked toward the spring just a little downstream. Then he turned and started walking toward One Eye.

"Well, Dad guessed that One Eye had enough sense to know not to let Amos get too close to him. If Amos had got close enough to grab him, he'd have broken One Eye in two. When Amos got about 70 or 80 feet from him, One Eye casually folded his arms across his chest, then quick as a cat, he flicked out that short-barreled .44, and it sounded like one shot rang out.

"The slug from Amos' gun struck One Eye about the middle of the chest and slammed him back against the rock. Both of his arms were flung out and the short-barreled .44 went sailing from his hand. Then he crumpled to the ground with a look of startled astonishment on his face. He was dead just about when he hit the ground.

"Amos just took a step backwards and stood there a moment. He put his gun back in its holster, half turned toward the camp, and then slowly slumped to the ground. Harvey and Ramon were softly cursing. Harvey said, 'I knowed I should have shot him when he crossed the spring … had my rifle on him.' Amos just looked at Harvey. Ramon cut away his clothes, and they saw that One Eye's slug had struck fairly close to where the ricocheted slug had struck the kid, about the middle of the stomach.

"Someone ran and got some blankets. They eased him on a couple of blankets, and six or seven of them lifted him on the blanket and carried him up to where the wagons were. Amos bore his pain stoically, but you could tell by his eyes he was hurting badly. Ramon tried to see if he could get the bullet, but all he had was a wide-bladed knife, and he couldn't do any good. Curley had a little bit of tequila left; he gave that to Amos, who drank it while Harvey lifted his head. He lived until nearly morning. All the men stayed around him wanting to give him what assurance they could, yet knowing there was nothing they could do. Amos knew he was not going to make it. Shortly before he lapsed into unconsciousness, he looked up at Harvey and whispered hoarsely, 'You look after Rosita and the kids, please, my friend.'

"Harvey swallowed hard, nodded and said, 'That I will, boss, that I will.'

"Amos died without a struggle. They buried him just north of the camp site as it was breaking dawn. Ramon, Harvey and Alfredo were crying broken-heartedly as they filled his grave, and most of the other men's eyes were wet, too. They piled some sandstone over him, then they started to break camp.

"Harvey was telling the men where to ride when he noticed One Eye sprawled against the sandstone. He hesitated a moment and then said simply, 'We can't leave him there, but we ain't burying him here.' So Alfredo put a loop around his feet and drug him about a mile from the spring. They scraped out a shallow hole and covered him up.

"Calhoun rose early on the morning the herd was due in. He knew they were on time as some of the older stock had led the way and had arrived at the near pasture the day before. About noon the main herd started coming in, and the air was filled with dust and flies and bawling cows and calves, but it was still three hours or more before the riders appeared pushing the stragglers before them, and you could begin to hear their staccato yells as they brought the cattle along.

"When the wagon appeared, Calhoun saw at once that Amos and One Eye were missing. He immediately spurred his horse, forcing him through packed cattle, until he reached Harvey's wagon. Harvey stopped his horses when he saw Calhoun coming and waited. The hands watched as Harvey told Calhoun what had happened, and when he had finished, Calhoun dropped behind the wagon and followed them up to headquarters.

"Rosita and her two boys were standing by their adobe door when Calhoun walked up and told Rosita. She put an arm around each boy and hugged them real close to her as she looked up and listened to Calhoun.

"Dad worked a year for Calhoun after that. He worked on other ranches and finally came north up here and got a chance to read law. He said that within six months Harvey married Rosita. They had a wedding right there on the ranch. Harvey moved in the adobe with Rosita, and Ramon moved into the cook shack. Calhoun seemed like he lost his spirit to a great extent after Amos was killed. Lots of times they'd hear him mutter, 'It's my blame, it's my blame, I knowed I shouldn't have took him on.'

"About three months after the drive a couple of federal marshals rode up looking for One Eye, and they seemed mighty relieved to hear that he was no more. They said he'd killed three lawmen, as well as several others in the territory, and they were mighty surprised to hear that a man with a hip draw had stayed even with him.

"Alfredo and Dad corresponded for some years after Dad left, and Alfredo wrote that Calhoun took Harvey in as a partner not too long after Dad left. He conditioned it that Harvey would turn it over to Amos' boys when they became big enough to handle the ranch. Calhoun died not many years after. Before he died, he made Harvey promise to bury him by Amos, and that's what they did. Rosita sewed a couple of blankets about him, and they drove him out to Sandstone Spring in the wagon and buried him beside Amos. All of the men went out, along with Harvey and the boys. Rosita said she couldn't go."

The door opening startled me, and I turned, half expecting to see Harvey, Alfredo or Ramon, but instead it was the circuit clerk who stuck his head in and said, "Judge, the prosecuting attorney says he's ready to take that plea when the court is."

The old judge was immediately brought from the far away and long ago to the present, and he responded with a "Very well, very well."

He arose and left the room, and Judge Green and I soon left the courthouse and drove back to our town. As we bumped along, Judge Green resumed pointing out places and houses, naming the people and cases with which they were associated. Just this side of town he pointed to an old house site and said, "See that clump of trees over there? That's where Grandfather's old homestead was. You know he fought in the Civil War for the North. Have I ever told you how he was captured by some bushwhackers?

"Well, before he went into the army he hadn't really taken sides, but his sympathy lay with the North. There was a bushwhacker named Bill McKee who came up from Arkansas and led a bunch of renegades in robbing and looting the countryside. They caught Grandpa out plowing, took his horses, tied his hands, put a rope around his neck and made him walk behind a fellow on a horse. That night they tied him to a tree and told him they were going to hang him in the morning. Then those renegades got to drinking and going through the loot they had stolen and didn't pay much attention to Grandpa. He was able to work loose from his ropes. He slipped over to where the horses were tied, untied a horse and mounted it as carefully as he could so as not to make any noise. As he threw his leg over the saddle, however, it hit a sabre that had been tied on the saddle, and it made a rattling noise. When this happened, this Bill McKee let out a whoop and yelled, 'The prisoner's loose,' and came running toward Grandpa with his pistol in his hand.

"Grandpa drew the sabre, and when McKee got next to him and started to level his pistol, Grandpa cut down on him with that sabre. He could have cut his head in two, but McKee saw the stroke coming and sort of stepped back. The sabre slashed right down his face, through his right eye and cheek. Then Grandpa spurred his horse and got out of there. The rest of the gang never even chased him. He rode back home and got his wife and children. They packed their things and started for Rolla that night. Grandpa thought he killed McKee, but later on he heard he'd recovered and joined a bunch of renegades down in Indian Territory."

Charley

YOU CAN NEVER TELL where the road you take in life will lead. Take Charley, for instance. Charley had it made until he decided he wanted more glamour in his life. If he had been able to look down that glamour road, knowing Charley, I don't think he would have taken it. But having taken it, for a few fleeting moments it brought out a quality of sterling character Charley had not had the opportunity to display before.

I don't remember when I first met Charley. It was probably during the summer of '36 or '37. His sister Violet was in my high school graduation class of '36, but I didn't meet Charley until after our graduation. Violet was a popular and vivacious girl who was always ready for a good-time party. She was an accomplished ballroom and tap dancer. Charley was a year or two older than Violet. He had graduated in '35, then went to Kansas State to study veterinary medicine. At that time Missouri did not have a veterinary school. Charley had been reared in town and didn't know, as far as I know, anything about the farm or animals. I don't think he even had a dog. I never could understand why he chose this particular field, but I guess it must have been that there weren't very many veterinarians around at that time and he thought the field had promise. I never asked him though.

At that time not many high school graduates went on to a higher education unless their folks had money. Charley's father was deceased, and his mother supported herself and the two children by operating a beauty shop. Violet didn't go to college, so Charley must have received the bulk of the family's accumulation and earnings to go out of state to veterinarian school.

I don't remember how I first met Charley either. I may have met him through Violet. She belonged to a girls' club along with a number of the popular girls in town, and they would often frequent a local night club known as Cozy Grove. They didn't serve mixed drinks at Cozy Grove, but there was a liquor store annexed to one side of the building, and you could buy alcoholic drinks and bring them into the dance hall area and then mix your own drinks. Charley didn't dance much as I recall, but he loved to have a few drinks and socialize among those who did dance. I never did see him drunk, but he generally had a bottle of whiskey he would share with you, along with the latest risqué jokes. He was jovial and generally well liked. He must have worked away some during the summer, but he would show up now and then for a party or two. Violet would always call him "Brother" instead of Charley. When she would see me and say, "Did you know that Brother is in town?" Or "Brother was asking about you," I'd know that Charley was in town for a few days and we would get together.

Charley didn't gamble or smoke. He liked a few drinks and he liked a few girls, but he was never serious about any of them that I knew. Charley was just a fun fellow. If he ever had a serious thought, you would never have known it. He was a rather irreverent person. I had the impression that he never took anything in life very seriously. Charley was not one to discuss philosophy, religion or history with. You discussed with Charley where you could get a date or a drink or who was having a party. I remember one night at Cozy Grove Charley was singing an irreverent little ditty when Jody James called him down and told him she didn't appreciate hearing it, that it was irreverent. Charley just laughed it off, but he stopped singing it. Charley wouldn't intentionally offend anyone.

I didn't go to college the same year I graduated from high school, but stayed on the farm until the fall of 1939. Every summer until then, Charley and I would get together several times during the summer. Sometime during the summer of 1938 we had a neighborhood rodeo at my brother-in-law's place, and after the rodeo Charley looked me up and we went out together. That was the last time I saw Charley for some time. I went to Missouri University from the fall of 1939 until the spring of 1941. Then I went to California. I was there when war was declared, and in 1942 I joined the navy flight program.

In the early part of 1943 I was taking flight training in Livermore, California, when Charley came to see me. I don't know how he had located me as we didn't correspond, but one morning I received notice over the public address that I was to report to the Commander's office. I was a bit apprehensive, but when I arrived, to my surprise, there was Charley, and he was a captain and flying A20s in the Army Air Force. He was the same old Charley, and he was ready for a party. He told me that he had already arranged for Barbara Davis, a home town girl who had married a California boy and was living in San Francisco, to get him a date, and all I had to do was get one, and we'd take in San Francisco.

This was on Friday, and I couldn't get off until Saturday, so Charley arranged to pick me up Saturday morning. He spent the time from picking me up at the Livermore base until we arrived in San Francisco bringing me up to date. He had graduated from Kansas State with a degree in veterinary medicine. When the war started, he had a chance to enter the army as a veterinarian with the rank of captain. He did so and was assigned to an Air Force base to inspect the meat being used by the personnel there. It was a deep cushioned job and left Charley with quite a bit of time on his hands. Charley, being a gregarious and likable fellow, became acquainted with a number of the flight officers, and they began inviting him from time to time to take rides with them when they were flying.

He said the first time he went up he was pretty frightened, but after several times he began to enjoy it. The more he was around the flying, the more dissatisfied he became with the mundane job of inspecting meat, so when he learned he could take pilot training and still keep his rank as captain, he took it. He received his wings and was now flying A20s, a medium attack bomber, and had been practicing low-level bombing and strafing missions in the desert by their base. The word was that they would be going to England to do low-level missions prior to the invasion.

We had a good time in San Francisco; we danced with the girls, had a few drinks and took in a couple of shows. I went back to the Livermore base Sunday evening. That was the last time I saw Charley. I followed him only in bits and pieces as one does in times of war, a fragment from some mutual acquaintance, or a rumor here, a newspaper clipping there.

His outfit went to England and they flew A20s across the channel and bombed and strafed the coastal defenses in low-level attacks preparatory to the invasion. They had the facetious saying that if they flew above tree-top height they'd go on oxygen.

The European coast across from England was heavily fortified, and these low-level attacks encountered devastating losses. Charley was one of them. His plane was hit at an altitude too low for anyone to bail out, but Charley, using the momentum of the plane and all his strength, managed to get the plane up to about 600 feet and hold it long enough for two of his crew to bail out. Charley went down with the plane, and his two crew members became POWs.

Posthumously, Charley received several medals, and these were sent to his mother. Some 58 years later, Lois and I went to St. Louis to attend our grandson's wedding. Just before we left to return home, I looked up Violet's telephone number. She had moved to St. Louis from Rolla after her husband passed away. Lois called her and she was delighted to hear from old friends. I talked to her a bit and mentioned how much I thought of Charley. She said she knew we were friends and knew of us getting together in San Francisco. She said when she moved to St. Louis she didn't know what to do with Brother's medals, so she gave them to one of her grandchildren. Charley would have liked that.

Buford

I MISS BUFORD WASHINGTON. I would never see him much in winter, but come spring, summer and fall you could see him nearly every day somewhere on the south side of the square. I can never remember seeing him on the north side. Generally, he was on the southeast part, east of South Main. His favorite spots were close to Aid's or the Red Apple Drug Store. He nearly always wore the same felt Stetson hat, although in the hot summer he did have a little faded blue colored straw he would wear. When I first became acquainted with him, he smoked a pipe, but in later years I don't remember him with it.

The first time I remember seeing him was down at the old County Farm close to 60 years ago. Elmer Dix ran the County Farm, and Buford had married Elmer's daughter Amy, and Elmer and he were going deer hunting in the fall. Buford was giving Elmer advice. I don't remember now what the advice was about, but it doesn't matter. Buford was always giving advice on something, and I can remember that Elmer didn't seem to be paying much attention.

Buford was a slim fellow with blue eyes and dark

hair. Later as he became older the dark hair was flecked with gray. He was a painter by trade and a philosopher by choice, and he usually wore the clothes of his trade. His happiest days were spent when there was some work taking place on the north side of the square.

Work fascinated Buford. He could watch it all day long and never seemed to tire. He could sit on the south side and direct your attention to the inefficient manner in which it was being conducted. This was especially so if the work happened to be painting, for of all his expertise, Buford had no doubt that he had reached the pinnacle of his chosen profession. He could quickly point out where the fellow was using the wrong type of brush, the wrong kind of paint, was making his strokes too long or too short, wasn't cleaning his brush in the right solution, or taking breaks too frequently. He was convinced that the workmanship was so shoddy it would give the profession a black eye. That was the reason people were reluctant to improve the looks of their property by keeping it properly painted, sloppy work like that.

Although painting was his forte, he was a skilled critic of about any type of craftsmanship or even manual labor. Any type of work seemed to fascinate him, and he could tell you all sorts of ways that the person or persons doing it could do it better.

He had a pretty good grasp of world affairs, too, current events, the decline of our culture and government waste. Understand he didn't stand on the street corner and blab about these things, you had to engage him in serious conversation to get these opinions. He was such a fixture there on the square that Russ Cochran put his picture on the front of the periodical printed about West Plains.

I recall his wife, Amy, as a nice-looking woman. They had two or three children. Amy and the kids left town when the kids got big enough, and I believe they went to Iowa where Amy got a job, but Buford and she never divorced. You might say they carried their fussing on by correspondence.

When they first married, they had a small house on the south side of town. There weren't any other houses within a couple of blocks of where they lived, and there weren't any roads to the south of them at the time. I think they got city water, but they didn't have any indoor plumbing, so they built their outhouse to the south of their residence with the door opening to the south. This provided proper privacy until the highway department built the bypass around town. When they built the bypass, they made a fill and laid the road about 15 or 20 feet above Buford's house just south of the outhouse, so the door opened to the highway.

Amy and the kids were gone, so it really didn't bother Buford that much. As the city grew and houses were built closer to Buford's, several of the new homeowners petitioned the city council to make Buford hook onto the city sewer system. They claimed it lowered the value of their new houses to have a neighbor so close still using an outhouse. But Buford pointed out to them that he was there before the ordinance was passed requiring sewer hookup, and the council decided Buford was grandfathered in and didn't require him to hook up to the sewer. He considered this to be a major victory over bureaucracy.

One day I went to town and Buford was sitting in the front of Doc Gardner's office. I stopped to talk to him and found him to be puzzling over a personal problem of some magnitude. It seems he hadn't been feeling well, and realizing that he was mortal, he wanted to prepare for his demise. He had secured a double cemetery plot in the Howell Valley Cemetery for Amy and him. He had ordered a double headstone with both of their names engraved. He had written Amy, who was now in Oklahoma, and sent her a bill for half of the cost of the stone. She had written him back and told him she wasn't sure that she wanted to be brought back here for burial. This created a dilemma of sorts for Buford. He already had the stone sitting in the front yard of his house. He had to decide whether to have the stone cut in two or leave it as it was and take a chance Amy would pay him her half.

I took my brother-in-law to see him on one occasion. They had been acquainted for years. We saw the tombstone sitting there in the front yard. It was a rather long stone and had Buford's name engraved on one end and Amy's on the other. They were situated where the stone could have been cut in two and made into two individual stones, although the names wouldn't have been centered. We noticed that the house was badly in need of painting.

I believe that's the last time I ever saw Buford. I read in the paper about his passing, and not long after that I read that Amy too had passed away. My wife's people are all buried in the Howell Valley Cemetery and we go there often. On one of our last trips there, I noticed that Buford and Amy's stone was in place and there were two fresh mounds, so I guess they solved the dilemma.

I've driven around the bypass and noticed that no

Buford

one has moved into Buford's house. I heard that one of Buford's children is fixing the house up. I saw that it has been painted, but I don't know that Buford would approve of the paint job, and the door to the outhouse has been left open.

The Demise of Lester Foutch

ON THE 10TH DAY of July, 1936, Lester Foutch, an oil field worker from Mountain View, Oklahoma, departed this life unexpectedly and abruptly when a bullet from a .45 caliber shell entered his left eye, ranged slightly upward and came out the back of his head. Lester was 30 years old, a rather young age to leave this world and step into the uncertain, ethereal afterlife. Fate and poor judgment on his part had made Lester's death more incongruous, due to the fact that the bullet wasn't really meant for him. It was meant for his cousin, David Burns, who providentially had left the coupe they both were sitting in but a minute before to go into the Pirnack grocery store in West Plains, Missouri, to buy some meat.

M.B. Burns, David's father, a hard-scrabble farmer from Oklahoma, had moved his family from Oklahoma to Missouri some time before the shooting to a farm in Howell County near the hamlet of Olden, Missouri. David, 27, who had a family of his own, followed his father, and brought his wife and three children. They rented an apartment at Five Oaks in the Heinrick apartments in West Plains about five months before the shooting. David's wife was expecting another child. David was eking out a meager living operating a miniature photo shop. He had taken his coupe, a single seated automobile popular in the late '20s and early '30s, to the Howell County Motor Company's garage on Washington Avenue to have a break on one of the fenders welded a month or two prior to the shooting; then he left and made a trip back to his old home in Oklahoma. When he returned, he brought his cousin Lester Foutch with him.

Lester was unattached at the time. He had worked in the oil fields of Oklahoma, had roamed around the country a bit, had been thwarted in an attempt to commit a robbery of a grocery store in Kansas using a baseball bat as a weapon, had served a few months in a Kansas jail for this infraction, and was among the vast army of the unemployed at the time he came with his cousin David to West Plains. In Kansas he had gone under the assumed name of Les Lester.

Both David and Lester were rough, hard-bitten sons of the great depression that had the world in its grip at the time. They had grown to adulthood in a poor country during harsh times, neither expecting nor receiving empathy from their fellow man. They reciprocated in kind.

When David returned to West Plains after his Oklahoma trip, the fender on his coupe had another break, and he took it back to the Howell County Motor Company and demanded they repair it again free of charge, claiming the break in the fender was a result of poor workmanship on the prior repair. Lester accompanied his cousin David to the garage to lodge the complaint. Austin Lambert was the shop foreman of the Howell

County Motor Company. After looking at the fender, Austin pointed out to David that the original weld had not broken; rather, the fender had broken in another place, but not as a fault of the garage's repair. Austin told David they could not weld it again free of charge.

David was adamant. He had learned that intimidation worked better than logic at times and this was one of those times. He began to denigrate the workmanship of the Howell County Motor Company in a loud and offensive manner. Lambert, taken aback by such tactics and wanting to avoid trouble and a scene, offered to reduce the cost of the additional repair by one-half. This act of pacification on Lambert's part only caused more vituperation from Burns. He saw that Lambert was giving ground, and he shoved all the harder. He not only castigated the shoddy workmanship of the garage, but began to cast aspersions as to the ancestry of the Amyxes who owned the garage and of Lambert himself. He had the pungent vocabulary of an oil field worker and the volume of a tornado alarm, and he was beginning to enjoy intimidating Lambert. It was at this state of the proceedings when Ray Amyx came into the garage.

The Amyxes were citizens in West Plains. Sid Amyx, the father, was a well-known politician and businessman in the adjoining county of Ozark. He had served as the State Representative of that county several terms in the Missouri legislature, and he owned and operated the Ford agency in Gainsville, the county seat. Four of his sons had moved to Howell County and lived in West Plains.

Ray, the oldest of the four, was in partnership with his youngest brother, Lyle (nicknamed "Pete"), in the

Howell County garage which they operated in conjunction with their Ford agency, a used car lot and a filling station. It was a popular hangout in the town. It was a place where you could play a game of pitch, hear the latest gossip or news — whichever you chose — get a drink of whiskey when you were dry, or just loaf and socialize.

The other two brothers in West Plains were dentists, each with their own individual practices. Lawrence, in his early thirties, was slightly built; his older brother Clay was heavier, and they were generally referred to as "Little Doc" and "Big Doc." Both had excellent reputations as skilled dentists, and Clay had served on the State Dental Board. Lawrence, although his skill as a dentist was well recognized, had the reputation of being a little on the wild side. He was not adverse to taking a drink and sharing one with a patient to numb the pain. He had an attractive little wife named Lenny. Lenny was inclined to be a bit jealous and on one occasion disturbed the social equilibrium by chasing Lawrence around the town square with a little pistol when she suspected him of stepping out on her. Generally, the local citizenry forgave these little foibles quickly. The Amyxes were well liked by the community.

It was hot and dry the summer of '36. The country was still in the throes of the depression. The coming election was the main thing of interest. Money was scarce, so all of the local offices had a number of candidates. The contest of sheriff had attracted five of them. Ray Amyx was one of the five. Ray was probably the most popular of the candidates.

Ray went into the garage where Burns was intimi-

The Demise of Lester Foutch

dating Lambert without really being aware of what was taking place. Burns immediately recognized Ray to be a person in a much better financial position than he was. This aroused all the pent up bitterness he felt toward anybody who wasn't on the lowest rung of the financial ladder with him. He verbally turned on Ray with a vicious, profane tongue-lashing. Ray was taken aback, but he recovered quickly and let Burns know in no uncertain terms that he was not about to get a free repair. The argument became more heated and Burns attacked Ray.

Amyx was in his forties and not experienced in fighting and not in the best of physical condition. Burns was 27, lean, strong, and an experienced street fighter. Ray was knocked to the floor. Now Burns didn't fight by the Marques and Queensbury rules. After he knocked Ray down he kicked him, then jumped on top of him, and proceeded to beat and bite him. He had nearly bitten one of Ray's ears off when Wilburn Duggan Griffen, an employee of the Amyx filling station, came to Amyx's rescue and pulled Burns off of him. Burns promptly knocked Griffen down, breaking his nose and rendering him unconscious. Van Cochran, an employee of the garage, came to Amyx's aid and knocked Burns down. Both Burns and Foutch then turned on Cochran, but when Cochran grabbed a tire tool and other employees came to Amyx's aid, Burns decided that discretion was the better part of valor and both Burns and Foutch headed out of the garage. Dr. Lawrence Amyx came into the garage just after the fight was over. Burns bantered Lawrence to fight with him, but Lawrence avoided a confrontation.

Since Ray Amyx had been badly beaten and one of

his ears nearly bitten off, he was taken to the Christa Hogan Hospital where his wounds were dressed and was taken home where he went to bed to recuperate. Even though Burns had unjustifiably and brutally beaten Ray Amyx, there was the possibility that the explosive situation could have been defused if Burns and Foutch had demonstrated a modicum of intelligent remorse. It was not to be.

Instead of leaving the vicinity after the beating of Ray Amyx, Burns and Foutch rather brazenly purchased some gasoline from the Amyx filling station, and one of them was heard to say, "I'll get that son of a bitch before the sun comes up in the morning."

News of the fight spread through the town and country like wildfire. Not many years before, the county sheriff had been slain by Alvin Karpus, a member of the Ma Barker gang with Oklahoma roots. Memories of Bonnie and Clyde and Pretty Boy Floyd gangs from the Cookson Hills of Oklahoma were still vivid. Burns and Foutch were unknown, but they were from Oklahoma, and with no justification Burns had viciously beaten a businessman who was liked and respected by the community in general. Public sentiment quickly turned to hostility toward them, a factor that played mightily in the events which followed.

The evening of the beating of Ray, Lyle Amyx had gone to the apartments where David was staying and vented his anger at Burns, daring him to come out. David was either not at home or declined to come out, as he failed to appear.

Lawrence had a little nickel-plated .32 caliber semi-automatic pistol. Lyle had traded an automobile a short time back to Andrew Cavaness, caretaker of the local army barracks, and in the trade had received a semi-automatic .45 caliber pistol.

Burns and Foutch had poked a hornet's nest. Within two hours of the fight, their every move was being observed and duly reported either to the Amyxes or as titillating gossip up and down the street. They seemed to be totally oblivious to the precarious position they were creating for themselves. The day after the fight Burns and Foutch drove in Burns' coupe out past Ray Amyx's house and past the garage several times. This was duly observed and reported to the Amyxes. They went back to the Amyx filling station, bought some gasoline and made sarcastic remarks disparaging the work of the garage. They were overheard to say, "They think they are damned smart, but we come from a country where we kill 'em." Someone else reported hearing them say, "We'll kill them before the sun goes down." The threats were quickly reported to Dr. Lawrence Amyx and Lyle.

The Amyx brothers were a close-knit family. Ray was dearly loved and respected by his brothers. They were not people who were ordinarily involved in fights, but they were on home ground and were not about to be bullied. As the activities of Burns and Foutch were reported to the Amyxes in the morning and throughout the day of July 10, and in view of the vicious beating that had been rendered Ray, both Dr. Lawrence and Lyle became convinced that a confrontation with Burns was inevitable. They were not going to sit back passively and let it happen. They were going to take the offensive.

A short time after 9 p.m. on the evening of July 10, Lawrence and Lyle were in the Howell County Motor

Company garage when word was brought to them that the Burns coupe had passed the garage, turned into Cleveland Avenue and stopped at the Pirnack grocery store which was directly across the street from the garage. The brothers immediately got in Lawrence's car, which he quickly backed out of where it was parked and pulled across the street by the Burns car on Cleveland. It was dark by then, but a street lamp at the intersection on the corner of Cleveland and Washington Avenue by the Pirnack grocery gave some illumination to the scene. A sense of impending drama saturated the area as a thick fog, and a number of people had already gathered to follow the Amyx car.

Providentially, immediately after Burns coupe had parked on the south side of the Pirnack store, David Burns had left the car and had entered the store through the southwest door, leaving Foutch alone in the coupe. When Lawrence Amyx stopped his car, he jumped out and confronted the only one left in the Burns' car, which was Foutch. Lawrence stood on the running board on the south side of the car and began reaching in and pistol-whipping Foutch with his little .32 pistol, while at the same time striking him with his other fist. Foutch was turning toward the north side of the car to avoid Lawrence's blows, when Lyle reached in from the north side as Foutch had his face turned toward him and shot him in the left eye with his .45 pistol.

When the shot was fired, the bullet passed through Foutch's head with its energy nearly spent, struck Lawrence in the breast, glanced on a rib and followed the rib around under the skin, exiting out the back. It was later found where it had expended in the street.

Lawrence realized immediately what had happened, and that he was not seriously injured.

Howard Morris, a West Plains city police officer, was making his nightly rounds just prior to the shooting, and was standing across the street at the back of Richard's store when he saw Dr. Lawrence's car turn into West Cleveland and saw a number of people running toward it. He could tell something was happening, so he started over. When he was about halfway across Washington Avenue, he heard a shot fired. About halfway between the front of Pirnack's store front and the door on the south side, he met Lyle Amyx trying to get the .45 pistol into his pocket. Morris grabbed Lyle's hand and Lyle tried to jerk loose, so he grabbed his other hand and retrieved the pistol.

Shortly thereafter Dr. Lawrence Amyx came up and handed Morris a .32 automatic pistol, saying, "I shot a man and he shot me." Lyle said nothing. Upon examining the pistols, Morris determined that although both gun barrels were dirty, the .45 caliber had been fired since it smelled of burnt powder and the .32 did not.

Morris took the Amyxes around to the car where Foutch was shot. He was dead and had a car crank in his lap. Morris didn't have a flashlight, so he felt around in the car and found nothing. He borrowed a flashlight from bystander Gus Jolliff and still found nothing. While he was looking in the car, Lyle left him and went back to the garage. Finding nothing in the car, Morris took Dr. Lawrence back to the garage.

Sheriff Ed Threlkeld had arrived, and Lyle and Lawrence's wives were there. Lawrence's wife was concerned about his wound, so Morris and Threlkeld took Lawrence to the Christa Hogan Hospital. There his

THIS I REMEMBER

wound was dressed and he was examined by Dr. R.E. Hogan. At the hospital, when Morris picked up Lawrence's shirt to examine it, Lawrence became defensive and told him to leave it alone. Morris reminded him that he was an officer of the law and had the right to examine the shirt. Morris was surprised to discover that although the shirt had two holes in it, Lawrence's undershirt had no holes at all.

David Burns, whose actions the day before had precipitated the shooting, was in Pirnack's store purchasing some meat when he heard the shot. By the time he went outside and discovered what had occurred, his cousin Lester Foutch was in the car either dead or badly wounded. Morris and the Amyx brothers had already gone to the garage.

Burns asked Antone Leamons to ride with him and show him where the hospital was, so he could take Foutch to the hospital. Antone, a close friend of Ray Amyx, refused, so Burns persuaded another spectator to ride with him to the hospital, where Dr. Hogan pronounced Foutch dead. He could not detect any powder burns on either Foutch or Lawrence Amyx.

West Plains night officer Joe Martin received word of the shooting and arrived in company with the coroner, Paige Robertson, just as Morris was taking Lawrence to the hospital. Martin examined the pistols and from the odor of burnt powder determined that the .45 caliber had been fired and the .32 had not.

An expended bullet from a .45 caliber pistol was found by Joe Martin just south of where the Burns' coupe had been parked; and Bunk Crider, another West Plains police officer, found a .45 caliber casing in back of the seat of the coupe. Dr. Lawrence had confessed to the shooting, claiming he shot in self defense; but he had a .32 caliber pistol, and the evidence indicated it had not been fired. Lyle remained silent, but a .45 caliber pistol, which smelled as if it had been fired, had been taken from him by Officer Morris. It had been examined by another officer who determined from the smell of burnt powder that it had been fired. The only bullet found was from a .45 caliber pistol, and a .45 caliber casing was found in the back of Burns' coupe. Dr. R.E. Hogan, who had examined the wounds of both Foutch and Dr. Lawrence Amyx, determined both wounds were caused by a bullet from a medium to large-sized pistol.

Whereas on the morning after the beating of Ray Amyx, the mood of the citizenry had been to prosecute the perpetrator; now, after the shooting of Foutch, they were suddenly confronted with a killing which they didn't care whether it was solved or was not. The Amyxes were well liked and the victim had the taint of an Oklahoma badman.

However, it was necessary for a law-abiding community such as theirs to at least appear to dispense justice fairly and impartially. Both Amyx brothers were charged with murder, placed under the heavy bond of $5,000 each, and released. As sort of a counter balance, David Burns was charged with felonious assault and placed in jail for lack of bond.

The shooting of Foutch had provided Burns with a very quick education. All of his belligerence had evaporated, and he realized the gravity of his situation. He was a one-man island surrounded by hostile waters. He had deliberately walked up to a pool of alligators and jumped in. He desperately wanted out.

Unexpectedly, the dilemma facing the local officials of the law came to his rescue. Floyd Bean was the county prosecuting attorney. He had two problems to contend with in prosecuting the Amyx brothers for murder. The first one was personal; the Amyxes were his friends. The second was congenital; he was by his nature a weak prosecutor. Yet prosecute he must in the interest of fairness. To demonstrate the integrity of the law, there had to be at least a show of vigorous prosecution.

There is no greater charade than that played in the legal system when both sides want to obtain the same results, while pretending a valid contest exists. It requires a certain degree of finesse to create the appearance of honesty, while concealing the underlining thread of deception. The first move on the chessboard was made by Bean. It was an artifice that created the impression of fairness towards Burns and the Foutch family. Bean dismissed the felonious assault charge against Burns, and he was released from jail.

A coroner's inquest was held by Coroner Paige Robertson on Monday, after the shooting on Friday. Prosecutor Bean assisted the coroner. Of the several eye witnesses to the shooting, none of them were called to testify. Only three witnesses were presented to the coroner's jury: Sid Garrison, Antone Leamons and Dr. R.E. Hogan, none of them eye witnesses. Sid Garrison and Antone Leamons sold cars from time to time for Ray and Lyle Amyx. Dr. Hogan had examined Foutch and Dr. Lawrence Amyx after the shooting.

Although Officer Morris had given a clear and detailed statement of the events leading up to Lawrence and Lyle's arrest, Bean chose to ignore his statement and placed Garrison and Leamons on the stand. Both testified that they heard two shots very close together. Garrison testified that he thought it was a car backfiring. The first thing he knew about any trouble was when Dr. Lawrence Amyx came past him holding his left hand from which blood was streaming.

"I'm shot," Garrison testified Dr. Amyx had said. Just then he saw Dr. Amyx's brother, Lyle, coming across the street from the garage. When the two brothers met, Dr. Amyx said to his brother, "Here, take this gun." Garrison said he then went over to the automobile in which the wounded man was sitting. Just then another man came up on the south side of the car and said, "This is my car, where is the hospital?" Garrison said that he did not know the man's name, but that it was one of the men who had been in trouble with Ray Amyx in the garage late Friday afternoon. Garrison said that he got in the car and drove away. He said that as he drove away he saw something thrown from the car, but he did not know what it was. Garrison also testified that he was at the Amyx garage Friday afternoon after the trouble occurred between Ray Amyx, Foutch and Burns. He said that Foutch and Burns drove up and down the street in front of the Amyx garage three times, and once they stopped and purchased some gasoline and one of them said, "I'll kill that son of a bitch before morning."

The testimony of Antone Leamons was practically the same except for a few minor details. He said he heard one of the men say as they were buying gas, "I'll get that son of a bitch before the sun comes up in the morning."

Dr. Hogan testified that both men were shot by a

medium to large-sized gun. He saw no powder burns on either Dr. Amyx or Foutch.

Representing the Amyxes was attorney G.W. Rogers of Gainesville, Missouri. General Rogers, as he was called, was thin, small of stature, wore ill-fitting clothes, and altogether was exceptionally unimpressive in appearance; but, his deceptive appearance concealed a razor sharp mind and a keen perception of human nature. He questioned the witnesses at length. The Amyxes were not present at the coroner's inquest. David Burns was. Dr. Hogan was asked the question by one of the jurors as to whether both Foutch and Dr. Lawrence Amyx could have been hit by the same shot. He replied that he couldn't say without knowing the positions of the two men when the shot was fired.

The jury was out only ten or fifteen minutes before they returned their verdict that Foutch came to his death from gunshot wound inflicted in a manner unknown to the jury.

Burns was the only relative of Foutch at the inquest, but several of his brothers arrived later on in the day. As a result of the coroner jury's findings, they decided to employ another attorney to assist prosecutor Bean. They hired Leonard Newton, an attorney in Mountain Grove, Missouri, as special prosecutor to assist Bean, much to Bean's relief. Thinking they were adding strength to the prosecution, they were unaware they were merely diluting responsibility in an unpopular prosecution and actually diminishing the chances of a conviction.

Preliminary hearing for the Amyx brothers was set for the 22nd day of July. By that day the defense had acquired additional attorneys: Dick Green, Bill Rob-

The Demise of Lester Foutch

ert and Homer Reinhart, all of whom represented all of the practicing criminal attorneys in West Plains.

The hearing was to take place in the old Methodist Church building. The county courthouse had been condemned a few years back after an explosion just off the town square had rendered it unsafe, and at that date it had not been replaced. This was before air conditioning; and although the heat in the make shift courtroom was nearly unbearable, the room was packed with spectators. This was before television had reduced the courtroom drama to the mundane, and local interest was at fever pitch.

Attorneys General Rogers and Dick Green were the lead attorneys for the defense. Dick Green was the antitheses of General Rogers in appearance. Green was large, well built, rather handsome in appearance and well dressed. The antitheses ended with their appearance. Green was more than the equal of Rogers in his mental acumen. He had a keen and calculating legal mind and was an excellent judge of human nature. In addition, he was accomplished in courtroom theatrics. The hearing was before Justice of the Peace William Luna.

At the onset, defense attorney G.W. Rogers announced that Dr. Lawrence Amyx would admit firing the fatal shot, but would prove it was done in reasonable and necessary self-defense. They petitioned for a continuance, setting out that they were informed that the slain man had a reputation as a turbulent, quarrelsome and dangerous character; that they had not had time to investigate the facts fully and obtain evidence relating thereto; that reports from the Department of Justice in Washington, D.C., to which Foutch's fingerprints were sent, showed that Foutch had been arrested in Independence, Kansas, in a grocery store robbery, and that he had been arrested in Anadarko, Oklahoma, and that when he was arrested in Kansas he had been going under the name of Les Lester. They believed that firearms were used by the slain man in the Kansas grocery store robbery; that inasmuch as witnesses cannot be compelled to come from other states, it would be necessary for council to go to the other states and take the deposition of numerous witnesses.

Attorneys for the defense argued that it was necessary to obtain the facts concerning the slain man, as they expected to introduce witnesses to prove that he was a turbulent and dangerous character, accustomed to carrying firearms; and, that Foutch and his cousin David Burns had, a few hours prior, beaten, bitten and kicked Ray Amyx (brother of Dr. Amyx and Lyle Amyx); and threatening the lives of the Amyx brothers, had driven to the home of Ray Amyx and had parked for a while in front of his home. This had been done after Amyx, who was badly beaten, was taken to his home late in the afternoon. Then, as an essential to the defense of their clients, the defense asked that the hearing be continued to enable them to check on the character of the slain man.

Although prosecutor Bean and his assistant Leonard Newton had anticipated the defense's request for continuance, knew it was reasonable and had actually desired it, this gave them an opportunity to make a great show of objection for the benefit of Burns and the Foutch family. They played it to the hilt. They vehemently and bitterly opposed any continuance, knowing full well at the onset that the Justice would grant it. Their objections and arguments waxed long and loud for a couple of hours, much to the entertainment of the spectators. Justice of the Peace, William Luna, who was in charge of the hearing, granted the defense a continuance of the preliminary hearing until the 12th of August.

On the 12th day of August the litigants appeared again and this time the State requested a continuance. Both the state and defense council had made trips out of state to Oklahoma and Kansas to take depositions of witnesses. The defense was ready for hearing. This time it was the defense council's time to object. The prosecutor and his hired assistant expected an assistant from the Attorney General's office to help them, and he couldn't be present on this particular date. This presented another excellent opportunity for the attorneys to put on a show for the benefit of the crowd, both sides knowing full well that the Justice of the Peace would grant the continuance. Both sides were well aware that an Assistant Attorney General in the case would further dilute the responsibility of the prosecution, and this was the unspoken desire of both sides. The hearing was continued to the 27th day of August.

What had started as an effort on the part of David Burns to save 75 cents on the welding of a break in a fender had spun completely out of control. He was now being carried along like a chip on the flood of events that he had precipitated. The attorney that he and his relatives had hired to help in the prosecution didn't give him that much assurance. The prosecutor and his attorney were just too nice to him. When they requested the assistance of the State's Attorney General, it indicated to Burns that they were unsure of themselves and the success of their prosecution. The Justice of the Peace, William Luna, was showing him too much deference, and this heightened the suspicions that already enveloped him as a blanket. He had no friends or acquaintances in the area he could council with. He could sense the hostility of the crowds that had gathered in the courtroom toward him. He was uncertain as to where to turn. Feeling he had to do something and not knowing just what to do, he and his relatives decided to ask their attorney to request that another Justice of the Peace sit with William Luna in the hearing. The request for another Justice to sit in on the hearing came as a godsend to William Luna. Both the Amyxes were his friends. He would not have to bear the sole weight of the decision as to whether or not to bind the defendants for a felony trial. He quickly granted the request and called his friend and fellow Justice of the Peace, J.C. Featherston of Brandsville, to sit with him in the hearing. Once again responsibility had been diluted so no single person would have to bear the responsibility of the ultimate decision.

On August 27th the courtroom in the old church building was jam-packed, and even at nine o'clock in the morning the heat was stifling. The Honorable J.E. Taylor of the Attorney General's office had arrived the night before to assist Prosecutors Bean and Newton with the prosecution. All were set to go. The prosecutor had two assistants, there were two judges and four defense attorneys. The stage was set. The audience, sweltering in that stifling heat, would have warmed the heart of any producer. No amount or kind of personal discomfort would deter them from sitting out the full length of the show. The crowd was overwhelmingly supportive of the Amyxes.

Seventy-one witnesses had been subpoenaed (24 for the state and 47 for the defense), an adequate number to assure enough confusion of testimony to justify any theory of the case. The morning was taken up by all the usual legal maneuvering and posturing that is such a hallowed part of the practice of law. The faithful spectators, dripping with perspiration, followed every part of the drama with fascination. They were living in that innocent age when the minds and imaginations of the public had not been tainted and dulled by the incessant rain of legal trials currently available on television.

It was 1 p.m. before the hearing began. The state laid out the evidence that would prove that Lyle Amyx fired the fatal shot with a .45 caliber pistol that killed Lester Foutch; that no other shot was fired; that the shot that killed Foutch traveled through Foutch and struck Dr. Lawrence Amyx who was standing on the opposite side of the automobile at the time with a .32 automatic pistol that had not been fired; that no other gun was found at the scene, either in Burns' car or on the persons of Burns or Foutch or in the vicinity. The testimony of Dr. Hogan established that both Foutch and Amyx had been shot with a bullet of medium to large size.

Dick Green gave the opening statement for the defense and told the court that Dr. Lawrence Amyx would admit to firing the fatal shot; that he fired in self-defense after he had been shot in the side by Foutch; that there had been two shots so close together as to seem to some to have been one shot; that the dead man's gun had been removed from the automobile during the few moments that intervened between the shooting and the time the car was searched.

The prosecution's testimony, which started at 1 p.m., continued until past 10 p.m. Few witnesses actually saw the shooting, but one who did was Frank Maumagh, a World War I veteran, and he gave a detailed description. Maumagh said that he and his wife and a friend were driving down Washington Avenue when they saw David Burns and Lester Foutch come up the avenue in a coupe and turn onto East Cleveland, where they parked their car near the back door on the south side of the Pirnack store. He said one man got out and went in the back door of the store, leaving the other man in the car. Maumagh said that he stopped his car at the Amyx station and that Dr. Lawrence Amyx came down Washington Avenue in his car, right behind him, but turned across the street and drove up East Cleveland where he stopped his car near the Burns' coupe. Maumagh testified that both Dr. Amyx and Lyle Amyx got out of the Amyx car and went up to the Burns' coupe; and that he saw the crowd going across the street, so he and his friend followed them. Maumagh said he saw Dr. Lawrence Amyx on the south side of the coupe striking at the man in the car. He said Dr. Amyx was striking at him with a gun which he held in his right hand and also struck at him with his left fist. Then, as the man in the car was turning away to avoid Dr. Amyx on the south side, Lyle Amyx, standing on the north side of the car, pulled a pistol out of his pocket and reached in and shot the man in the car. There was only one shot fired. When pressed for details by Dick Green on cross examination, he said that Foutch was leaning back toward the north side of the car trying to get away from Dr. Amyx's blows.

"Then how," said Attorney Green, "do you account for the fact that Foutch was shot in the eye and the bullet came out the back of his head the way it did?"

"Why, Lyle just retched in and shot him," Maumagh retorted.

At Maumagh's statement, the huge crowd of spectators roared with laughter and the Justice had to rap his gavel repeatedly to restore order. He demanded the audience keep quiet.

Officer Morris testified how immediately after the shooting he had apprehended Lyle trying to get a .45 automatic pistol into his pocket, and about that time Dr. Lawrence Amyx came and handed him a .32 automatic pistol and said, "I just shot a man and he shot me." Morris said the .45 smelled as if it had been discharged and the .32 did not. Officer Martin testified about finding the .45 caliber bullet just south of the Burns' car in the street, and Officer Crider told about finding the .45 caliber casing inside the Burns' coupe. All of the witnesses called by the state testified that there was just one shot fired.

After the prosecution rested, the case was continued until the next morning.

The defense witnesses far exceeded the prosecution both in number and variety and imagination. Some of the defense witnesses testified that they saw the Amyxes walk across the street to the Burns' car. Some testified one of the Amyx brothers was on the south side of the car. Others put the same brother on the north side. One testified that Lawrence handed the gun to Lyle after the shooting, and all of them testified that two shots were fired so close together that it sounded like one shot.

One of the defense witnesses was in the expert category. This was Captain Moore, firearms expert with the Highway Patrol. Captain Moore was examined in a sly way. The .45 caliber bullet which had been found by officer Martin had been compared with a bullet fired from the .45 caliber taken from Lyle Amyx. Ballistics showed that the bullet found came from Lyle's gun, Moore testified. However, neither the prosecution nor the defense had bothered to have the .45 caliber casing found in the Burns' coupe tested to see if it came from Lyle's pistol. Instead, Attorney Green asked Moore if he had an opinion as to whether or not the casing had been fired by the pistol taken from Lyle. He gave his opinion that he believed it did not due to the angle of ejection of the .45 automatic. He said the .45 would eject its casing 135 degrees to the rear, but the casing was found in the back of the Burns' car.

This aided the defense theory that another gun had been used in the shooting, although none was ever found. All the evidence was that Foutch was shot with a larger caliber weapon than the .32 used by Dr. Lawrence Amyx.

The defense witnesses, together with the arguments of the attorney, lasted all day and far into the night. The partisan audience that packed the old courtroom, profusely perspiring in the oppressive heat, savored every word.

Finally by 10 p.m. the justices took the case for decision. *The West Plains Daily Quill* duly reported the decision.

"At the close of one of the most unusual preliminary hearings ever held in Howell County, Justice William Luna of West Plains, and Justice J.C. Featherston of Brandsville late last night announced they found the evidence insufficient to warrant binding Dr. Lawrence Amyx and his brother Lyle Amyx over to Circuit Court on a charge of murder for the slaying of Lester Foutch on July 10th. Throughout the long hearing the courtroom was packed with interested spectators who had endured the sweltering heat in the poorly ventilated courtroom in the temporary courthouse to hear the testimony and the argument. When Justice E. Luna announced the decision, there was a lusty cheer by the crowd.

"Assistant Attorney General J.E. Taylor of Jefferson City, who was sent here to assist the prosecution of the Amyx brothers, stated in his argument last night that the case is the most unusual one in which he has ever been employed, and the most unusual one which he has ever known. Although the defense attorneys contended Dr. Lawrence Amyx, 32-year-old dentist, killed Lester Foutch, the state contended the fatal shot was fired by his younger brother, Lyle Amyx, 23, member of the Howell County Motor Co."

After announcing the findings, the two Justices quickly departed the courtroom by the back stairs. The prosecution offered its condolences to David Burns and the Foutch family. The Foutch family left the next day to go back to Oklahoma. Ray Amyx resigned from the contest of sheriff resulting in the election of Claude Garrett. David Burns, subdued and much wiser, stayed on in Howell County. Time covered the scars of his early indiscretions, and forty-five years later he was elected a county commissioner of Howell County for a term of two years. Ray Amyx and Dr. Lawrence Amyx both passed away at a fairly young age. The older brother, Dentist Clay Amyx, served honorably as mayor of West Plains for a number of years; and Lyle Amyx, always respected and well liked, owned and operated a popular national resort noted for its hospitality. Time marches on.

The Trial of Riley Tooley

RILEY TOOLEY WAS A happy man. He was a large man, so whenever that salubrious mood enveloped him, there was quite a bit to be happy. Riley had a one-gallus sawmill operation by the Eleven Points River, and he lived adjacent to his sawmill. His customers consisted mostly of a few neighbors who needed rough lumber from time to time, but his main source of income was selling ties to the railroad. Toad Brody was his helper. Sometimes when business was booming, he hired a local neighbor to help Toad. Riley had a reputation for being a fairly honest man. When you sold him a patch of timber, you could count on the fact that he wouldn't cheat you much on the scale.

Riley was also a good fisherman. He had been born and reared on the Eleven Points and he knew the river like the back of his hand, where the deepest holes were and where was the best place to catch goggleye, bass (small or largemouth), or jack salmon, useful things like that. The truth of the matter was that he preferred fishing on the river to sawmilling, but the drawback to his preference was that you have to sawmill once in a while to buy gas for the johnboat.

Everybody who knew Riley liked him. They were his friends. However, the winds of change were floating in the air. Some fellow from the city had put a big piece in the Sunday section of the St. Louis paper about the beauty, peace and quiet of the Ozark stream, and now more folks from the city were running down on the weekends to see where that beauty, peace and quiet was. As a rule they weren't fishermen. They were canoeists mostly. You could hear them talking loudly and making noise on the river some time before they came and passed your fishing spot. They were usually friendly folk and didn't bother too much. But they brought game wardens. They didn't even call themselves game wardens any more, but Conservation Agents. It used to be that you bought your fishing license and that was it. Nobody bothered you, and next year you might buy a license again. Now, though, you'd see one of those fellows every once in a while. They wore little uniforms like they were law men, and some of them even wore law men hats. But that was all right just so long as they didn't bother anyone fishing.

Today was a beautiful, sunshiny morning in May. Word was that the trout were biting below Greer Springs about as fast as you could throw your plug in the water. Riley had shut the sawmill down. Toad and he had split the cost and filled a chest full of ice and beer, gassed up the johnboat, loaded the minnow bucket and fishing gear, and were headed up the river for Greer Springs. Their hopes ahead and their cares behind, no one could ask for more. Riley was a happy man.

The morning mist was still hanging over the water as they headed the johnboat upstream. Toad was in the front of the boat and Riley ran the motor. It was several miles from where Riley lived to Greer Springs, so Riley pushed the ancient Evenrude to its limit, as he wanted to pick a good fishing spot before someone else beat him to it. The trip was pleasant and uneventful. Riley and Toad were the first to set up on the riverbank just below the bridge that spanned the stream and about 100 yards below where the spring entered into the river. The cold water coming from the spring sustained trout for some distance, until the warmer waters of the river gradually warmed the spring waters.

When it became public knowledge that the stream was good for trout fishing, it began to attract fisherman from the cities and surrounding areas, so the state started stocking the area with trout on a regular basis. The stocking days were quickly noted by the local river men, and the news traveled faster on the river than on the telegraph. It was in response to this word that Riley and Toad were brought to this piece of fisherman's paradise.

They had both caught a couple of good-sized trout and had consumed an equal number of beers before their first competitors arrived. They were neighbors, a father and son who lived about half a mile below Riley and would buy lumber from him from time to time. There was the usual salutation of "How's fishin'?" and Riley and Toad proudly displayed their catch to the envy of the new arrivals. The neighbors politely motored upstream a respectable distance from Riley's spot and began casting. Within an hour or so a half-dozen other boats, whose occupants were all known to Riley, selected places either above or below Riley and Toad's spot.

Conversation carried clearly over the water, and you would hear the shout of someone from time to time as they hooked a good keeper or the mumbled complaints of those who lost some or had to throw one back that was too small. Riley and Toad were having good luck, such good luck, in fact, that they were having to consume more of their beer than they had anticipated to make room for their catch. They had consumed all but one can of their beer and had their limit of trout, and there was a good-natured debate going on between Riley and Toad as to whom the last can of beer belonged. Before they were able to resolve their dispute, a pleasant young man in a new boat eased up to their spot and asked them how the fishing was going. He eased his boat into the bank in a courteous manner, got out and introduced himself.

"Howdy, fellows, I'm Hugh Wilson," he announced in way of introduction. "How's fishing? I hear there's trout somewhere around here." He extended his hand, and Riley took his hand in the fraternal spirit of a brother fisherman.

"Name's Riley Tooley, and this here's Toad. The state put a bunch of trout in the water yesterday, and you can catch 'em from the spring all down the river 'til the water gets too warm," Riley replied in a friendly manner. Succumbing to the temptation to brag on their catch, which is the ban of fishermen the world over, he took the top off the chest to display their catch and added, "We caught a chest full already, looky heer."

Hugh Wilson was intensely interested in the trout. In fact, he was so interested he carefully counted them. Then in one terse announcement he burst Riley's bubble of joy like the shattering blow of a sledge hammer.

"Mr. Tooley," he said, at the same time producing a very official looking badge, "I'm going to have to ask to see your fishing permit. I am an agent with the Missouri Conservation Commission."

Riley was completely dumbfounded. It took his numbed mind a full 30 seconds to recover any degree of the functioning process. When his vocal cords did return, they returned with the bellow of a wounded bull.

"Hey, fellers," he shouted, "they's a game warden here pretendin' to be one of us. Watch out for him." With that announcement he ran to his johnboat, leaving Toad on the bank with the agent, while he proceeded up the river shouting in a voice that reverberated up the river and through the hills and hollows, shouting the warning that there was a game warden "amonst us pertindin' to be one of us. Be on guard." When he had motored past the spring, he turned his boat around and proceeded down river shouting the hue and cry, giving the warning to all who were fishing the trout waters of the spring. When he had completed this solemn duty, he motored back to pick up the faithful Toad, who was waiting with the rather perplexed agent for his return.

Hugh Wilson's training had never prepared him for an outburst of this nature with such proportions. There was nothing in the books attaching an offense to warning other fisherman that he was checking licenses, and he didn't quite know what to do, but he thought he had to do something. Besides raising an uproar about his presence, Riley had been shouting the hated words **game warden** at the top of his lungs. Although the two fishermen had only their legal limit, they had them in the same ice chest, and that violated the regulation about co-mingling their catch. Wilson had been unobtrusively carrying a bag in his left hand, and he quickly went to the ice chest and scooped the fish from the chest and transferred them into his bag. At the same time, he notified Riley and Toad in his most official voice that they were going to be cited for the violation of co-mingling their catch and were going to be summoned into court.

If the discovery of a spy in your camp wasn't devastating enough, they were now having their entire catch confiscated. Riley had never in his life faced a catastrophe of this magnitude. He felt his knees get weak and he had to sit down.

Hugh Wilson had been an agent with the Conservation Commission for only two months. He could still hear the stern advice given to him by his mentor, Phil Brechard, who had been an agent for a number of years.

"The worst offenders you'll find are the farmers and people who have lived on the rivers for years," he said. "They think the game and fish belong to them, and for years there weren't many game regulations. We have to teach 'em and show 'em when they don't pay attention, that the game and fish belong to the State, and we're the State. They're awful tricky, and sometimes you got to work undercover to catch 'em. But understand, the regulations of the Conservation Commission are your laws, and those are the laws you've sworn to uphold," he told the new agent with evangelistic zeal. "They may be the leaders of the community or even law men. They may be trusted by their neighbors and not steal or cheat in a trade, yet they'll take a bull frog from their pond out of season, or if their dog catches a gray squirrel in the woods out of season, they'll skin it and eat it without thinkin' there's one thing wrong with it. It's our job to catch 'em and to teach them to show respect for our laws. They think our laws are not as important as their laws. Do you understand?"

Hugh Wilson had listened with rapt attention and had nodded affirmatively. Brechard had continued his message with all the zeal of a motivational speaker at an Amway convention, "Sometimes you're all alone out there, you may not be appreciated by folks in general, but you're there for the good of mankind. You're there to protect the little animals, the squirrels, the rabbits, the deer and the birds and the fish. If it wasn't for you, they wouldn't be any of them left for your great grandkids. I can't impress on you too much how these creatures depend on your enforcing the regulations of the Conservation Commission." And he added, "Regardless of who it is and whether they are your best friend, remember, you're an officer with the Conservation Commission, you're not a game warden."

Brechard was zealous, idealistic and conscientious, which can be desirable virtues; but mixed in double proportions without the balance of wisdom and understanding, they can produce the opposite result of an intended objective. Wilson had this to learn.

Riley was at his sawmill when the sheriff came to serve him with the warrant for his arrest. He knew the sheriff well and had voted for him at the last election. The sheriff acted extra friendly and asked Riley how he was getting along, how the kids were, what the price of ties was now and how fishing was on the river before he got around to telling Riley he had a warrant for his arrest. He hastened to explain that he wasn't going to arrest him, but he needed to turn himself in to the Magistrate Court in the next day or two to make bond. He went to some length to explain that it was something he had to do, that in most game violation cases a summons was issued instead of a warrant, but in this case the Conservation Agent had insisted to the prosecutor that an arrest warrant be issued for Riley and a summons for Toad. He let Riley know that he wasn't in favor of these Conservation Agents slipping around and posing like they were fishermen. If he could help Riley, just let him know and not to hold this against him in the next election. After some small talk about how some of his neighbors on the river were, the sheriff left Riley to ponder the vicissitudes of life.

Riley was not a complicated man. His life was simple; his wants were few. He was married and his wife and he had three children. Their wants were few also. They all fished on the river, went swimming during the summer on the river, during fall and winter went turkey and deer hunting, went to Alton, the county seat, every other Saturday to get sugar, flour, meal and what other necessities were needed, and once in a while took in the movie theater. Life was predictable. Riley knew today what tomorrow would be like. Oh, there might be slight variations, but all in all he could easily visualize what two weeks from today would be like.

Suddenly and abruptly like a huge meteorite being hurled into a placid pool, life no longer reflected the mirrored picture it once presented. All the images were distorted. Riley needed direction, so he decided to seek out his friend, the sheriff, to see what advice he could garner from him. The sheriff had been in office two terms and had once lived on the river himself. He was going to run for office again and would want Riley's vote and, besides, Riley was well known and liked up and down the river. He would need that influence also.

Early the next morning Riley was in the sheriff's office presenting his problem to his friend who was more knowledgeable about these things. The sheriff listened attentively, and when Riley had related the events leading up to his encounter with the Conservation Agent, he offered his advice. "You understand, Riley, they're kind of law enforcement men and we have to sort of cooperate with 'em in enforcing their regulations. They ain't really laws, they're just rules they make all the time and keep changing. But we have to help 'em according to law even if we don't like some of the way they go about enforcing 'em." Then he gave Riley the name of a lawyer in an adjoining county he would recommend, and with that Riley took off for the lawyer's office.

It was about 9 a.m. when Riley reached the office. Riley had never been to a lawyer before in his short life. The lady at the desk asked who he wanted to see, and when he told her she asked if he had an appointment. He told her that he had just an hour ago gotten the lawyer's name and he hadn't talked to him before. She spoke a little bit on a telephone and told Riley he could come back at 10 and the lawyer would see him. Riley went out to his pickup and waited until the appointed time and went back into the office.

The lawyer was friendly and had an easy-going manner, and when he asked Riley to tell him what his problem was, Riley was beginning to feel a degree of assurance. He related the events leading up to his warrant in detail. He couldn't understand why every once in a while the lawyer would sort of chuckle. Even when he told about the game warden getting his fish, the lawyer kind of chuckled. Evidently, the lawyer never had any of his fish taken away, or he wouldn't have thought it so funny. After he had finished his story, the lawyer began to ask him all sorts of questions: Had he ever been in trouble with the law? How long he had lived in the area? How long he had been sawmilling? He continued asking how much he made and a lot of questions he didn't think were any of the lawyer's business, but he was good-natured about it, and somehow it was hard not to like him. After he finished questioning Riley, the lawyer announced he'd be happy to defend him for a $500 fee. Riley thought that was rather steep, but he agreed to pay, and the lawyer said he'd require at least $100 paid down. Riley wrote a check for the $100.

Then the lawyer called the judge in Alton, told the judge he was representing Riley, that Riley was pleading not guilty and asked the judge to set the case for trial. He also asked the judge to let Riley make his own recognizance. The judge agreed and the lawyer told Riley to go on back to Alton, report to the Magistrate Court's office and sign the bond. Riley did as he was told.

It was the fall of the year before the trial of the State of Missouri vs. Riley Tooley and Toad Brody took place in Alton, the county seat of Oregon County. The leaves on the trees were turning into a kaleidoscope of color. There was a tinge of frost in the air. Deer season was just around the corner. Ordinarily, it would have been a joyous time of the year for Riley, but his arrest had so upset the usual tempo of things as to cause the rhythm of his life to be in complete discord. He was ill at ease, but it helped him somewhat to see his lawyer taking everything so calmly. The lawyer seemed as if he actually was enjoying everything that was going on and knew what was taking place. He and the prosecutor were friendly, and the lawyer even spoke nicely to the game warden and called him Mr. Wilson.

The case had generated a great deal of interest among the river folk, so the courtroom was packed with Riley's friends and the curious who wanted to get a good look at the game warden who posed as a fisherman. The circuit judge who was presiding had been on the bench for a number of years and had acquired the wisdom that only comes with experience and an even temperament. The jury was comprised of local farmers, loggers and river men, and most of them had served on previous juries. The trial occurred at a time before television had captured and emasculated the legal profession, so the 18 citizens who had been summoned knew that their responsibility was to judge their fellow neighbor honestly and fairly in the same manner they would expect if their situations were reversed.

Six of the 18 jurors had to be eliminated to bring the number down to the legal 12, so both the prosecutor and Riley's lawyer questioned the jury panel to see if there was anyone either side wanted to strike. The prosecutor then took the list, struck off three of the names and gave the list to Riley's lawyer. The lawyer went over all the jurors with Riley to see if there were any that Riley had a particular interest in striking from the panel. He was acquainted with several on the jury, but he had no serious objection to any of them, so they handed the list back to the judge and told him they would accept the first twelve people on the list.

After the jury was sworn, the prosecutor made his opening statement and told the jury how Riley and Toad were caught red-handed with co-mingling their catch of trout. The prosecutor explained the purpose of the regulation was to keep people from cheating and allowing one person to catch more fish than his limit and giving them to someone else. He explained that it was an open and shut case, that they had their fish in one ice chest and not separated. He explained that they were caught by Conservation Agent Wilson, and that the fish would be introduced in evidence so the jury could see for themselves that it was an open and shut case, and that they had the duty under their oaths to return a verdict of guilty against the defendants and assess such punishment against them so as to deter others from violating the game and fish laws of the State of Missouri.

Riley's lawyer then made his opening statement and explained that Riley and Toad were just two hard-working sawmillers. He described in detail the backbreaking labor they performed in their little sawmill operation just to put food on the table for their families. He explained that they were honest, hard-working men who were the salt of the earth, that they would never cheat each other or their fellow man out of money or fish, that their sole recreation from their hard life was when they had a respite from their labors and could go fishing, that even then they scrupulously adhered to every jot and tittle of the law; that this case was not an instance of anyone violating any law or regulation of the State of Missouri, but a classic example of a young, zealous and inexperienced officer jumping to conclusions; that as the evidence unfolds the jury could see what a waste of the taxpayers' money, not to mention the onerous burden placed on these two sterling citizens, by the State bringing this frivolous case. Riley and Toad began to emerge as two overweight cherubim in bib overalls, and they were wearing their mantle of injured innocence well.

The prosecuting attorney then proceeded to introduce the evidence for the State. Agent Wilson was sworn in and proceeded to outline the details of his confrontation with Riley and Toad. He told of his opening their ice chest and counting the fish and then taking the fish from the chest and putting them in his own bag. The prosecutor drew a mass of frozen fish from a chest and asked Wilson if he could identify them. Wilson could and testified that those were the same fish he had confiscated from the defendants and preserved them for this trial. Then with an air of triumph the prosecutor placed the frozen mass on the judge's bench for all the jury to see. Riley in a hoarse whisper to his lawyer that could be heard over the courtroom said in an accusatory tone, "Them's our fish."

Riley's lawyer was very polite when he questioned the agent. He called the agent Mister Wilson, and asked him all about his training. He asked Wilson if he could tell the jury if there was anything in Riley's chest besides the fish, and Wilson said he hadn't noticed in particular, although there might have been one can of beer; no, the number of fish didn't exceed the limit for the two fishermen, but they were co-mingled. Then the lawyer said, "Of course, Mr. Wilson, you're not telling this jury that the fish were in a lump in the chest like the frozen lump on the court's bench are you?"

Mr. Wilson allowed that the fish were scattered out

unfrozen in the chest. He also confessed being agitated with Riley when he began shouting that there was "a game warden amonst us."

After the testimony of Wilson, the State rested its case and Riley was placed on the stand to give his testimony. He recounted the events of the day, told the jury how Toad and he were scrupulously honest with each other and would never think of claiming the other's fish. Then the lawyer asked him how they could tell which fish belonged to whom. Riley then explained that in their preparation to go fishing, they had neglected to throw the stringers in the boat and didn't notice until they tied up and had caught their first fish. They had solved the problem by placing the beer in the chest between the fish. By the time they had caught their limit they were down to one beer; but they had scrupulously kept that beer between their two catches until the game warden had mixed them all up. Now they'd just have to guess whose fish was whose, and he cast an accusing glance at Wilson.

The prosecutor on cross-examination tried to ridicule his testimony, but Riley stuck to the simplicity of his story, and when Toad testified he confirmed it.

In the arguments before the jury, the prosecutor heaped scathing ridicule on Riley and Toad's testimony, and Riley's lawyer countered with the sterling and unblemished character of the defendants. Then the jury retired to deliberate.

There is a nervous air of uncertainty and expectancy that envelops the court, the litigants and the spectators alike when a jury is deliberating the fate of an issue which has been placed before it, whether it be the guilt or innocence of a person charged with murder or a game violation. It differs only in the intensity. And so, when the sheriff announced that the jury was ready to return its verdict, a hush descended over the crowd as the jury filed in. The judge asked the jury if it had reached a verdict, and the foreman answered in the affirmative. Then the court asked the foreman what the verdict was, and the foreman declared both defendants not guilty.

The nervousness which had been gripping Riley and Toad burst with a flood of relief and exultation. Well-wishers rushed up to congratulate them. They in turn were thanking their lawyer and the jury. The confusion of the moment had so diverted their attention that they were not noticing Agent Wilson. As the jury read its fateful verdict, an ashen-faced Wilson had walked quickly to the judge's bench, seized the frozen mass of fish, grabbed the chest he had brought them in and dashed for the courtroom door before Riley noticed what was taking place.

The agent was going through the courtroom doors and was running down the stairs before the reality of what was occurring was absorbed by Riley's thought process. Wilson had taken the fish! When the full impact of this indignity struck him, Riley bellowed like a wounded bear, "Hey, them's our fish!" and he took after the agent. The agent, however, had too much of a head start and was in his pickup headed out of the square before Riley ever got downstairs. The order of the courtroom was in disarray, and the judge was tapping his gavel to restore order when Riley came puffing back up to the courtroom. The judge discharged the jury. Riley had won his case, but lost his fish. He was disconsolate.

Toad, however, was more philosophical in a practical way, "Good thing I didn't drink that last beer, Riley, you owe me one."

Skeeter

LOIS AND I WENT to Shoney's for lunch the other day, and as we were starting in I noticed a large, older model automobile parked near the entrance and recognized it as Flossie's car. Sure enough, when we walked around by the left door, there was Flossie sitting in the front seat behind the wheel. Her aunt, Bedie Oaks' sister, was sitting in the passenger's side.

When she saw me, she broke into a big grin and began getting out of the car. Flossie was a large woman in her late fifties with a dark brown complexion, an infectious smile and bubbly laughter.

"Why, Mista Moore," she exclaimed as she grabbed my hand," I jus' gotta get out and shake your hand. It's so good to see you. Mista Moore, did you hear Lige passed away? I went down to Oklahoma to his funeral Mista Moore, and they was a lotta folks there ..."

Lige Oaks, "Skeeter" as he was known, brought back a flood of memories. When I first started practicing law some 45 years ago, he worked at Woodworth-Cochran, the old Ford agency. He was a small, slender black man of about 19 or 20 years of age. He was quick in his actions, and that, together with his diminutive size, earned him the nickname of Skeeter, Skeet for short.

In the early fifties I represented the Ford agency and had occasion to be there frequently. Skeet and I became fast friends. Skeet lived on the "Hill" as the black community was known, and when any of the people had problems, Skeet steered them to me.

In the late summer of '51 I had a little office over the old bank building. We had no air conditioning in those days. The office faced west, and in the afternoon the sun shining on the brick building made the heat oppressive. It was into this atmosphere that Skeet brought Charlie to see me one afternoon.

I was not well acquainted with Charlie, although I knew he shined shoes sporadically at one of the barber shops on Washington Avenue. I also knew of his reputation for imbibing excessively in any liquid that had an alcohol content. Charlie was of medium build, stood about 5'9" in height and looked as if he had just crawled out from under a house. Charlie had lived a hard 30 years. He was content to let Skeet do his talking.

"Mista Dick, Charlie here, he were in an acseedent down 'bout Cauldfield when dat gasoleen truck turned ovah, and Charlie he was riding as a passanger. Now, Mista Dick, Charlie warn't bad hurt, he jus' kinda got his eyebrows singed off and he gots a few blisters on his face. He's all right now, ain't you, Charlie?" Charlie nodded in affirmation, "But Mista Dick, Charlie and me was kida wonderin' if maybe Charlie might be able to get a little of that insurance money 'cause it warn't Charlie's fault no way."

I told them I would see if we could collect anything from Charlie's injuries and took a statement from Skeet with Charlie's minimal help as to how the accident happened. It seemed as if Charlie was just along for the ride, when one of his buddies was delivering some gas to a station in Cauldfield. Charlie was unsure as to how the accident had happened, but it was a one-car accident with very few injuries. Charlie had not been to a doctor after the accident.

I explained to Skeet and Charlie that I would take the case on a contingent fee basis of one third of the recovery. As I explained this procedure, I directed myself to Skeet, and he in turn would explain to Charlie. "You see, Charlie, it's dis way. The man, he'll write the insurance fellow, and they'll kinda write back and forth to see if the man can get you some money, Charlie. It ain't gonna cost you nothing, Charlie, but if the man gets some money for you, Charlie, you gonna owe the man a third of what's you get. That okay, Charlie?"

Charlie had a blank look on his face. He blinked his watery eyes and stared in an uncomprehending way as if he were trying to solve a mathematical problem of some complexity.

"That okay with you, Charlie?" Skeet repeated.

"Uh huh," Charlie replied more out of faith than conviction.

After Skeet and Charlie left, I wrote the company which insured the truck, and after several weeks and several exchanges of letters, we arrived at a settlement figure of $3000. I sent for Charlie. It was in the afternoon when Charlie showed up looking the worse for wear.

"Charlie, the insurance company will pay you $3000 for your accident," I announced. "Of that $3000, I will get one-third." Charlie blinked his eyes and stared a moment, and I was reminded of the sunlight starting to penetrate a morning mist. His face brightened, and he replied, "Den I gets the fouth?"

I tried to explain to Charlie about the portion he would receive, and suggested that he authorize me to put his portion in the bank, and he could then draw it out monthly as he needed extra money.

Charlie replied, "Uh huh, unhuh," in a detached sort of way, and then brightly as if he had a sudden revelation, "Mista Dick, can I go gets Skeet, to splain dis?"

I assured Charlie he could go get Skeet, and he left. In about a half-hour the two of them came back. Skeet was the spokesman. "Mista Dick, Charlie hea don' quite undastan' 'bout the insurance money. Counds you tell me and I'll splain to Charlie, Mista Dick."

I went through the explanation with Skeet, and he kept nodding in affirmation. "Un huh, un huh," he agreed, "Charlie, the man he is tryin' to hep you, Charlie. You know, Charlie, long 'bout winter, hit gits a little thin, Charlie, and if the man puts yore money in da bank, Charlie, and you gets it along as you needs it, it'll hep you, Charlie. You understand, Charlie?"

By this time Charlie was nodding in agreement with a pleased look on his face.

"That okay with you, Charlie?"

"Un huh."

"Mista Dick, that's okay with Charlie, but right now, Mista Dick, we needs a hundred dollars."

"You know, Mista Moore, when Crocket died, Lige came up here to the funeral and they was lots of people came, and Lige said, 'Crocket had a nice funeral, I hopes I have as nice a funeral as Crocket.' And you know, Mista Moore, they was a lot of people at Lige's funeral, and as they was a putting him down, I says, 'Lige, you had as nice a funeral as Crocket.' He shore did, Mista Moore, Lige had a lovely funeral."

Ethics

The moril of this story, it is plainly to be seen:
You 'aven't got no families when servin' of the Queen —
You 'aven't got no brothrs, fathers, sisters, wives or sons —
If you want to win your battles, take an' work your
    bloomin' guns!
                    — Snarleyow-Kipling

AFTER 50 YEARS IN THE practice of law, I received this certificate from the State Bar Association congratulating me on my long and ethical career and service to the Bar and my community. It was a pretty certificate and signed by the President and Secretary of the bar with the official seal and all the trimmings. My wife said, "Isn't that nice!"

The next day reality set in when I received another letter, this time from one of the members of the Bar bureaucracy of the Continuing Law Committee. The letter reminded me in rather ominous terms that I had failed to complete my yearly requirement of three hours of legal ethics training. Ethics! I thought to myself, they have created a façade of false pretense and polite smiles and call it ethics, then require you to take a course in it to collect the fees!

Of course, it's necessary to have ethics in about anything you do, although the standards vary from profession to profession. For instance, I live in a trading community, and it's considered perfectly ethical to catch some newcomer who is unfamiliar with the values of commodities like cattle and cheat the daylights out of him. And in the real estate business it's considered downright unethical not to relieve a well-heeled buyer of a substantial part of his surplus cash.

You may not believe it, but there really are ethics in the legal profession — that is, sort of; they may be a bit different from what you learned in Sunday School, but if you look hard enough you'll find them. Take a fellow like Ben Searcy. Ben was a well-known and respected lawyer in Shannon County when I first started practicing law, who had tried all sorts of cases all over the circuit and adjoining circuits. Ben was noted for his honesty and candidness. If Ben told you something, you could make book on it; he later became circuit judge. I learned a great deal about legal ethics from Ben.

I was separated from military service in January 1946 after four years in the Marine Corps. I worked around for a couple of years and started studying law in 1948, passed the bar exam in 1951 and started practicing in April or May of that year. I rented an office over the old West Plains Bank building and furnished it with a couple of chairs, a typewriter and table that doubled as a desk. I tried a couple of no-fee cases in Magistrate Court, and around the last of May or the first of June a young fellow from Shannon County came up the stairs and wandered into my office looking for a lawyer. I assured him that he had come to the right place and learned he had been arrested for burglary and larceny in the town of Eminence. He told me that he had been arrested for burglarizing a shoe store and stealing a pair of shoes. He assured me of his innocence and asked what I would charge to defend him.

Well, you know a dollar was worth a great deal more back then than it is now, and I had never fixed a fee for a felony case, was dead broke and had no idea what to charge. Without figuring my time and gas expense or anything else I blurted out, "Thirty-five dollars."

Without saying a word, he pulled out some bills from his pocket and paid me thirty-five dollars. I noticed with chagrin that he had a number of bills left that he returned to his pocket. I then took the particulars of his arrest and whatever data he could furnish. He gave me a date in July that he said he was to appear in court. I wrote him a receipt and he left. I was floating on air. I had a real live honest-to-goodness client and thirty-five dollars burning in my pocket.

It was only a couple of days later that I was at the Howell County Courthouse where I met Boss Green, whom I knew to be the prosecuting attorney of Shannon County, and I told him that I was representing one of the citizens of his fair county. As fortune would have it, I also told him I was going to take a change of venue from the county. I had already learned that this was one of the standard things a lawyer usually does to stall a criminal case.

Boss Green was an affable fellow, up in years, and had been prosecuting attorney in Shannon County for a number of years, and it was to prove fortunate later on that I chanced to see him and give him that information that day.

We lived about 10 miles from West Plains in the old

farmhouse I had been born in. If you remember at that period after WW II, automobiles were in scarce supply and rather expensive. I had had my name on a list to buy a new auto at Paul Johnson's Chevrolet for some time, and along the last of June my time arrived. We bought a brand new 1951 Chevy. We didn't have a garage, so we had to park it outside, and we put on plastic seat covers to protect the seats. At the time we had three little kids.

You know time has a way of rolling around, and the day for my client's July court appearance was upon me before I knew it. I had assumed the date he had given me was for a docket call, so I was in no particular hurry. Docket call days at that time were when motions were taken up and lawyers jockeyed for position to try or to stall their cases.

I left home about 8 a.m. and headed for West Plains. Henry Hays who worked at Williams Shoe Store was a good friend of mine, and I had arranged to pick him up and take him with me to court for companionship; so after I stopped at my office to pick up my briefcase (which was my badge as a lawyer), I picked up Henry and we headed for Eminence, our hearts young and light.

At that time we didn't have air conditioning in our car, and as we traveled I began to notice a rather uncomfortable feeling where I was sitting. I pulled over on the shoulder of the road and explored the cause and discovered that one of our children had been playing in the car and had deposited his bubble gum on the plastic seat cover on the driver's side under the wheel. I had sat squarely upon it, and as the July heat combined with my body heat, it had produced a melting effect that assured a good bond between the seat cover and the seat of my pants. We stopped at a filling station in Winona, still several miles from Eminence, where Henry took his knife and did his best to scrape the gum off my pants, and we got some paper towels to put over the gum left in the seat.

It was then up in the morning, and it was about noon when we pulled up to the courthouse in Eminence. I walked into the courtroom with Henry trailing me. I was all smiles and confident of a welcome from the judge. That euphoria dissipated like a drop of water in a hot skillet when I saw the face of the judge and a jury sitting in their chairs, and suddenly realized that this was no docket call. This was a trial date!

I quickly learned that the jury and court had been waiting for me since 9 a.m. The state was ready for trial and the date had been set a month of so before; Ben Searcy had been hired by the complaining witness to assist Boss Green, the prosecuting attorney, in prosecuting the case. They were ready, the defendant was present, the jury and the court were ready. I had to fight a feeling of panic. My mouth got dry and I had the same feeling I had the first time I was catapulted off a carrier deck. I stepped up to the bench and said, "Your honor, I wasn't aware this case was set for trial, I had seen the prosecutor some time ago in West Plains and told him I was going to take a change of venue from the county." Boss Green acknowledged that this was true.

I was beginning to see a bit of daylight in the dark when the judge said, "Mr. Moore, do you have your change prepared?" Judge Gordon Dorris had been circuit judge for a number of years. He was a wise, fair and compassionate man, and he also realized the spot I was in, so he declared a recess so Ben could speak with me.

Ben took me aside and said, "Son, you don't have a change drawn up, do you?" When I acknowledged I didn't, he said, "Son, it don't take 15 minutes to take a change of venue from Shannon County. I'll have my girl draw one up in no time," and he dashed off across the street to his office and in about ten minutes came back with a change of venue from Shannon County. I felt like a drowning man who had been thrown a rope, but was not quite sure the other end was secure.

"Ben," I said, "I don't have any affidavits."

"Well, son, we'll take care of that," Ben says as he signed a couple of affidavits his secretary had attached with names I had never heard.

"What if Boss Green looks at the file and sees the affidavits are fake?" I asked.

Ben dismissed my inquiry, "Hell, son, he'll never look at the file." The judge granted the change of venue, and the case was sent to Oregon County.

In the trial which took place several months later, I made sure I was there on time. Ben helped Boss Green prosecute the case, and Ben gave a rousing speech to the jury for my client's conviction. Henry again accompanied me to the trial, but this time I was ready. The jury acquitted my client, and I never missed a court date again.

Now why would an experienced lawyer like Ben run the risk of committing two felonies just to keep an inexperienced lawyer who was his competitor in the case from being embarrassed in court? Ben was a compassionate fellow, but he could skin you alive in a case without flinching. I never could figure it out. Around this time I had filed as a candidate for the office of Prosecuting Attorney and I did get elected. Ben's practice was primarily in criminal work, and a great deal of his cases came from Howell County where West Plains is the county seat.

You know, after I took office I held it for a number of years, and when Ben was on the other side of a case and called me saying, "Son, I need a continuance," I could hardly turn Ben down.

Maudibel

WILLY ROUSE WAS A fellow you could pass by without hardly noticing. Oh, he was pleasant enough and he wasn't that bad looking — tall, blond hair, an easy smile. People generally didn't like or dislike him. You just couldn't take Willy seriously; and you were reluctant to do business with him, because you could never be sure just what Willy meant when he told you something. For instance, if he told you he would be over to help you in the morning, you couldn't be sure he was thinking of the morning of the same day you were. But he was always pleasant about any misunderstanding and just explained that it was a mix-up.

He was the sort of person who lived and died without causing much attention. Early in Willy's life, Willy's father learned the art of living off government programs. He had passed this knowledge and training on to his children, and Willy had been an apt student. At an early age, Willy had developed an aversion to any type of labor that caused one to perspire.

This created somewhat of a problem when Willy grew into a tall, lean, muscular adult. He could no longer qualify as a dependent child, and, when he could no longer contribute to the family income, he abruptly found himself on his own. This required a bit of an adjustment, but Willy knew the system, was friendly with social workers, spoke their language, and quite effortlessly became a tall, lean, muscular sick man.

The trouble was his back. It caused him excruciating pain when he tried any type of labor. After numerous hospital stays, X-rays and examinations, it was finally determined that he had a congenital back problem that, although unable to be specifically diagnosed, was disabling enough to keep him from being gainfully employed, and he was placed on disability income.

Willy, being a rather nice-looking fellow with a steady income from the government, was an attractive catch to several of the girls around Brownsville, so he could afford to be choosy. The problem was, though, in this area of life he had no experience, and his judgment was poor. He picked Debra, a smart, ambitious, buxom, dark-haired girl who was one of the better looking women in the village. Of all the alluring qualities of the female sex, beauty can be the most fickle, and intelligence is next. Debra possessed both, and it didn't take long for her intelligence to tell her that the government income from a disabled spouse wasn't going to provide the quality of life she had envisioned. Willy explained to her that she could get a job, and they could make it fine. So Debra got a job as a waitress, but then he discovered to his horror that when Debra began to earn a salary, the government cut his pension some.

About this time, Debra's other attribute attracted a traveling salesman who frequented the restaurant where she was supplementing the family income. The salesman left generous tips, and Debra began looking forward to his coming. The friendship ripened, and he began painting (and she began to envision) a picture of life that was much more colorful than the one she could see at the present. One thing that wasn't in the picture was Willy. One evening after she got off work, she was seen getting in on the passenger side of the front seat of the salesman's new Ford sedan and leaving without looking back. She left without saying goodbye to Willy. Willy was deeply hurt and offended, but he recovered quickly when his disability pension was increased to its original amount.

Willy was more astute in his next marital venture. He chose Maudibel, a hard-working farm girl who had been widowed early in life. Maudibel was the daughter of German immigrants. Her father and mother had emigrated from Germany right after the First World War. They settled on an infertile plot of land and worked hard to make a living. Maudibel had several brothers and sisters, and they all worked from daylight until dark to wrest a living from that infertile land. Maudibel had married an enterprising fellow who had a milk route, but in the first year of their marriage he was killed in an automobile accident. So Maudibel returned reluctantly to the family farm. When Willy began to show her some attention, she didn't think much farther ahead than to visualize that Willy might be a ticket to leave the farm. Her folks didn't approve of her marrying Willy, because they said he was lazy, and they told her she would have to support him. But Maudibel figured she wouldn't have to work any harder than she had and, besides, Willy said he had a pension they could live on. She didn't know how much the pension was, but it didn't take much for

Maudibel to make do.

They were married one winter day and Maudibel moved into Willy's two-room house in Brownsville. Willy ran out of wood to put in the heating stove the next day, and Maudibel used a chain saw to saw up a tree top and to load wood into the back of the car while Willy drove the car. Willy could drive the car, but his back illness wouldn't allow him to lift something heavy like a chain saw or wood. If his case worker heard of him using his back in this manner, he'd have to go for some more examinations. They might even take his pension away from him. So they played it safe. Maudibel did the heavy work, and Willy did the supervising. They managed to make it through the winter. Willy's pension fed them, paid the rent and the electric bill on the little two-room house. Maudibel cut the wood for the heating and cooking stoves.

Maudibel had often dreamed of a life where hard daily work was eliminated, but somehow now that she was experiencing it, she found herself thinking fondly of pitching feed to the cows, cutting sprouts and making fence posts. Doing nothing never seemed to bother Willy. Willy was always full of all sorts of ideas about making money. He used to tell her about some of them, and Maudibel was impressed with how complicated they were. It seemed to her, though, that none of them involved any work for Willy. He had thought about a laundromat that Maudibel could run if they only had money enough to buy the equipment, or a cleaning business in which she could supervise a crew who would be working for her. He could put in a restaurant that specialized in German food that she could run if they only had the money to put it in. Willy was sure it would make lots of money. Maudibel also couldn't help but notice that when they were inside, Willy didn't have any trouble lifting the heaviest sticks of wood and putting them in the heating stove, sticks that she had difficulty lifting. He was always talking about buying this or buying that when he got ahead a bit, and Maudibel began to realize that this was just Willy talking, and that he never intended to get ahead a bit.

One day he said he was going to buy a radio as soon as they got ahead a bit, and she could restrain herself no longer. She told Willy he was lazy, and that he wasn't smart enough to make enough to buy a radio without working, and he was too lazy to work. Willy left in a huff. He took the car and didn't come back until the next morning just before daybreak while it was still dark. Maudibel was just getting up.

Willy wasn't mad any more, but he was excited and nervous, and his clothes were messed up. He told her he had a calf in the back of the car, and she was to take it to the sale barn and put it in the calf sale as soon as she could. When she asked him where he got the calf, he told her he would explain that to her later. If anyone asked where she got it, she was to say she bought it off a fellow and to stick with her story. Then Willy said he had to go to bed, as this was the day the case worker was coming to check on them, and his back was hurting.

So when daylight was just breaking, Maudibel started to the sale barn with the calf in the back seat of the car. Willy had put some straw in the back on the floorboard so it wouldn't mess the car up so bad. She went to the entry gate and had to lift the calf out of the back of the car. The calf was a nice heavy newborn. It weighed over 100 pounds, she judged. The gate man tagged the calf with a number, took Maudibel's name and address, and gave her a receipt.

It was not quite 7 a.m. when he heard the cow bawling. Bill had just finished milking, so he took the milk to the house and strained it before he went to check on the cow. The cow had given birth to a calf a couple of days before, and Bill had put the calf and her in the small pen that was below the barn. It was a good place to isolate a fresh cow for three or four days before placing her in the herd again.

She'd had a good strong bull calf, and he would take it to the sale barn next week and it should bring a hundred dollars or more. The calf had probably slipped through the fence and the cow was bawling for it. The pen was about 150 yards below the barn, and the nearer Bill got the more he realized that cow was really agitated. When he arrived, he could see why. The calf was gone and the cow was frantically running around the pen and bawling at the top of her lungs.

It didn't take Bill long to deduce what had happened. The pen was adjacent to the highway. The highway was on a fill which elevated it 15 or 20 feet above the lot where the calf had been. It had been a wet spring, the embankment from the highway to the fence was soft, and there were two sets of footprints imbedded in the soft embankment, one leading from the highway down to the lot and the other, a bit deeper where the thief had struggled up the embankment with the extra load of the calf. The evidence was written so graphically that Bill read it instantly. Somebody else wanted that hundred or so dollars the calf would bring as bad as he did.

It was 9 a.m. by the time Bill had gone back to his house and driven his pickup to Alton where he could report the theft to the sheriff. The sheriff immediately contacted the Highway Patrol headquarters, and they in turn alerted Corporal Bobby Ousley who had not yet had his second cup of morning coffee at the local law enforcement's watering hole in the city of Thayer. The county prosecutor resided at Thayer, and inasmuch as cattle rustling ranked very close to capital murder in this part of the country, Bobby decided the prosecutor should be in on the investigation. The prosecutor did indeed want to participate in the investigation, so by 10 a.m., Highway Patrolman Bobby Ousley, the County Prosecutor, the Sheriff and Bill met at the scene to conduct their investigation. They quickly came to the same conclusion as Bill. Someone had stolen his calf.

Now, somewhere in some book on wisdom it is written that there is profit in many counselors, and such was the instance at hand. Someone asked Bill where he usually sold his calves, and Bill said the sale barn at West Plains. Another remarked that this was sale day there, and within seconds it was decided the investigation would adjourn and reconvene as soon as the delegation could get to the sale barn at West Plains.

West Plains was the regional market for livestock from the surrounding countryside. The cattle are segregated as to age, tagged, the seller recorded, and the cattle penned. There was a large pen full of bawling young calves, and this was the pen the law delegation was directed to by the accommodating sales manager. It took Bill some time to locate his calf, but locate it he did. The sale barn records revealed that the calf had been brought to the barn about 8 a.m. by a lady named

Maudibel Crouse. It didn't take long to locate Maudibel; she was waiting for the calf sales.

Maudibel had an interesting explanation. She had come to the sale barn to purchase a calf and was approached by a man who offered to sell her the calf at what she thought was a bargain price of $50, so she bought the calf and put it for sale, hoping to make a little money on the trade. Besides, how could Bill prove it was his calf anyway? There was only his word. The sheriff, prosecuting attorney and the highway patrolman couldn't identify the calf, could they? As Maudibel saw that they admitted they couldn't identify the calf, she became more aggressive. How dare they accuse her of stealing a calf when all they had was one man claiming he could identify a little calf out of a pen of 200 bawling calves! And he admitted he had just seen the calf a couple of times before.

Bill allowed that the cow would know if it was her calf or not, and Maudibel, recognizing that her position was becoming rather tenuous, offered only feeble objections. So the sheriff of Oregon County borrowed a pickup, and with an entourage consisting of the highway patrolman, the prosecutor, the sheriff and Bill, proceeded to Oregon County to introduce the calf to its mother. Both the calf and mother were delighted, and a warrant was issued to arrest Maudibel for felony stealing.

Three days later the warrant was delivered by mail to the sheriff of Howell County. He was aware the warrant was coming and had been investigating the theft. The sheriff knew both Maudibel and Willy. He knew Maudibel to be a hard-working daughter of German immigrants and Willy to be a rather unreliable fellow who was on a disability pension. It was the sheriff's thinking that somehow Willy had to be involved in the theft of the calf, so, before he would serve the warrant and arrest Maudibel, he wanted to check into Willy's activities on the day the calf was taken.

The sheriff had long suspected that Willy was a malingerer, so he went to inquire of his condition from the Division of Family Services. He was directed to Willy's case worker, a Miss Ethel Rentle. Miss Rentle was a lady in her late 40s. She had been a case worker for nearly 20 years. She loved the authority and prestige that enveloped her position in the eyes of her clients, and she had developed a feeling of omnipotence in her counseling and in her ability to discern whether or not the clients were being truthful with her.

Yes, she was very well acquainted with Willy Crouse. She had known Willy and his family for years. No, he was not a malingerer. He had a congenital back problem that permanently disabled him from any gainful employment. He truly wanted to work, but his back illness prevented him from holding a job. As a matter of fact, she could testify that on the day the calf was supposed to have been taken, she personally knew him to be sick in bed with his back as she had checked on him that very morning.

The sheriff rather reluctantly went by Willy and Maudibel's house and told Maudibel to come in to town the next day with her bondsman and he would serve the warrant on her. If she would bring her bondsman with her, she wouldn't have to go to jail.

Maudibel felt fear, betrayal and anger all mixed together. When the sheriff left, she turned on Willy, and for a few moments Willy was afraid she was going to physically beat him. She grabbed a stick of wood and descended on him. He displayed an amazing dexterity in jumping out of bed and in dashing out the door before she could bring the full force of her angry blow upon him. It was some time before Maudibel calmed down enough for Willy to talk to her, and talk he did. He cajoled, pleaded, begged and promised. He insisted it was like he had said; he got the calf from someone on the road. Maudibel told him he was lying. He knew he had to be at his persuasive best, so he put on the best performance he could muster. It was every bit as good or better than the one he had used with Ethel Rentle when he had convinced her he had this excruciating pain in his back when he did any work. Tears came into his eyes. Sincerity oozed from him in huge waves. He saw Maudibel begin to waiver and he could anticipate victory. He told her he would never intentionally do this to her, he thought too much of her. He just thought the calf had been a bargain, and she had been quarreling at him, and he thought this would be an opportunity to make her proud of him.

Maudibel finally dropped the stick of wood and began to sob. Willy put his arm around her and told her not to worry. Everything was going to turn out all right. She just had to stick to her story that she had purchased the calf from a fellow she didn't know, and the authorities couldn't prove she didn't. If she told them she had gotten the calf from Willy, they would claim that both were in on the theft. Willy would lose his pension and their livelihood. Besides, they could both land in jail.

Her parents, Hans and Anna, went her bail, both telling her that they knew Willy was responsible for

Maudibel

all the trouble. When they went to the sheriff's office to make bond, Willy didn't go with them. He said he was too sick with his back to travel in the car. The jarring of the road travel caused him such pain. Hans and Anna went with Maudibel to employ the lawyer. The lawyer questioned Maudibel by herself. He had her go over the events several times. He asked her to describe the man she purchased the calf from three different times; each time he made notations on a yellow pad. By the conclusion of the interview the lawyer was convinced of two things: one, Maudibel didn't physically take the calf; two, she knew who did.

The lawyer had been acquainted with Maudibel and her parents for a number of years. He knew them to be honest, hard-working people in the Brownsville community. He also knew Willy Crouse and his family background and immediately concluded Willy was lurking somewhere in the murky picture. He took the case, collected his fee from Hans and Anna and took a change of venue from the county, which would ensure a delay in the trial for at least three months and maybe more.

Maudibel went back to Willy and worried. Willy was the model of proper decorum. He even helped Maudibel load a little of the cook stove wood and he was awful nice to her.

The case was sent to Carter County for trial. Carter was the smallest county in the circuit, which meant the docket was not very crowded, and when the docket was called, the case would be set for trial rather quickly. Fortune, however, smiled upon Maudibel, for when the Carter County docket was called, the Oregon County prosecutor asked for a continuance as Trooper Bobby Ousley, one of his main witnesses, would be in federal court in Springfield and would not be available. Maudibel's lawyer breathed a sigh of relief. The juries in Carter County were notorious for their clear-thinking, no-nonsense approach to theft of any kind, and Maudibel's story of her purchase of the calf stretched the credulity even of her lawyer.

In the trial of most criminal cases the first line of defense is a continuance. Time generally works to the advantage of the accused, not always, but generally. Some of the witnesses move from the area or die, officers get transferred to another district, the prosecutor leaves office and becomes a defense attorney, memories fade, or some other hoped-for thing happens. Maudibel, however, had no such fortune. When the fall term of court rolled around, everybody concerned was still alive, the officers were still on duty, the prosecutor was still holding office, and Bill was still mad about someone stealing his calf. Only the cow, which was now expecting again, had forgotten the incident. At the fall docket call, Maudibel's case was the first called and set for trial about a month away.

The prosecuting attorney and Maudibel's lawyer were well acquainted and had a friendly rivalry going. Maudibel's lawyer himself had been a prosecuting attorney of the adjacent county for a number of years. The prosecutor was of the opinion he had an open and shut case, and Maudibel's lawyer knew that another continuance was out of question. The prosecutor hinted he would recommend a light sentence if guilty plea was entered, inasmuch as Bill had recovered the calf. The lawyer duly conveyed the information to Maudibel and she refused the offer. Both sides prepared for trial.

It was a warm fall day in October when the trial

was held in the old courthouse in Van Buren. The jury was interrogated and selected. Six men and six women, honest citizens of Carter County, were duly sworn to determine the guilt or innocence of Maudibel. Maudibel was pale, tense and terrified. She was dressed modestly and looked smaller than usual. Willy was feeling too badly to attend the trial.

The prosecution was confident of a conviction. Cattle theft was a grave offense to these small town farmers on the jury. There was the indisputable evidence that the calf belonged to Bill's cow and that Maudibel had sold the calf at the sale barn in West Plains. That evidence had been enough to bind Maudibel over to circuit court on a felony charge. On the defense side, there was only Maudibel's unsubstantiated story that she had purchased the calf from a stranger she couldn't identify. Maudibel's attorney was apprehensive. The state had just put two witnesses on the stand at the preliminary hearing, the sales barn checker, who had checked the calf in from Maudibel, and Bill, who testified that the calf on being brought back to the cow was his and that the cow verified this when she accepted the calf. Maudibel's lawyer figured the state would have two more witnesses, the sheriff and the corporal of the highway patrol. If these two could tie the tracks down the embankment to Maudibel, all was lost.

The lawyer decided to waive his opening statement until the end of the state's evidence, so the prosecuting attorney outlined the state's case to the jury. The prosecutor told how Bill had heard his cow bawling and upon investigation had found the calf gone and the cow agitated. He told how he had seen the tracks coming down from the highway to the cow and calf's pen and the tracks going back which were deeper, indicating that the person going back up the embankment was carrying the calf. He told that this would be verified by Corporal Billy Ousley of the highway patrol and the sheriff of Oregon County, that the man from the sale barn would identify Maudibel as the person who delivered the calf to the sale barn, that Bill had identified the calf among about 200 head of calves brought to the barn, and the calf on being taken back to the cow was accepted by her and allowed to nurse.

The lawyer noted that the prosecutor had not connected the tracks with Maudibel in his opening statement and heaved an inner sigh of relief. Could it be that no one had measured the tracks going down and up the embankment? The impressions had been deep and could have been easily taken. The state's witnesses proceeded to testify in the order as outlined in the prosecutor's opening statement. Maudibel's lawyer offered little in the way of cross-examination, but as the evidence progressed it began to be evident to him that none of the witnesses would testify as to the size of the footprints leading down and up the embankment.

The prosecuting attorney was confident of a conviction. The table where both the defense and prosecution sat was parallel to the jury. Both the defense council and the defendant sat on the side next to the jury, and the prosecution and complaining witness sat on the opposite side. The prosecuting attorney was sitting at the front of the table on the prosecution's side. He was leaning back in his chair in a relaxed manner with his legs crossed as he was questioning the witness and was moving his leg and foot back and forth. The prosecutor was a good-sized man with a fairly large foot, and Maudibel's lawyer noticed from time to time that several of the jury's eyes wandered over to the prosecutor's foot as he questioned the witnesses.

The last witness of the prosecution to testify was Corporal Billy Ousley of the Missouri State Highway Patrol. Corporal Ousley was a large and impressive-looking officer. He had spent a number of years in the army before coming on the patrol and had the reputation as an honest and sincere officer. He was not, however, experienced at testifying in court. The defense lawyer could detect he was nervous.

Corporal Ousley duly recited the evidence which had been given by both Bill and the sheriff, how tracks came down from the highway to the pen where Bill's calf was and then the tracks went back up the hill to the highway. But there was still no connecting the tracks to Maudibel.

The prosecutor was still rocking his leg and foot back and forth when the defense started cross-examination. "Billy, what size were those tracks that came down the embankment and then went up it?" asked the lawyer. The question caught Billy by surprise, and he nervously glanced at the prosecutor's foot. The lawyer quickly suggested an answer, "About the size of the prosecutor's foot?" Billy seemed happy and relieved that the answer was so simple, and he replied, "Yep."

At Billy's "Yep," the prosecutor became unglued. He jumped to his feet, and forgetting Billy was his witness, he shouted, "I object." Then, realizing his objecting was out of order, he withdrew his objection. In the meantime, the jury was examining Maudibel's small foot in comparison to the prosecutor's.

The jury foreman was a lady, and she smiled at Maudibel as the jury returned to the courtroom. Maudibel looked as if the weight of the world had been taken from her shoulders when the foreman pronounced the verdict "not guilty."

Hans and Anna came running up, and Hans in his practical way shook his finger at Maudibel and said, "Shee now, you get rid of Villy, before he shteals another calf!"